Praise for *From the Core*

"*From the Core* is for every struggling, determined, distracted, beautifully powerful man that you know—which is to say, all of them. This is urgent. Clearly. John's insight supports men to grow into the active healers and heart-centered leaders that the world needs."

Danielle LaPorte
author of *The Desire Map* and *How to Be Loving*

"John's work and his words have changed my life, and this book is no exception. John has a brilliant way with words that make sense of our experience, lead us to grow and step into our fullest potential, heal what needs to be healed, and not just understand what healthy masculinity means but also how to be it and live it. John is a gift to the world, and this book is a gift to yourself. Buy it."

Mark Groves
human connection specialist and founder of Create The Love

"*From the Core* is a masterpiece and guidebook for anyone who's looking to level up their lives. John beautifully weaves together big concepts into easy-to-understand stories and practical lessons that can be applied immediately."

Preston Smiles
two-time bestselling author of *Love Louder: 33 Ways to Amplify Your Life* and coauthor of *Now or Never: Your Epic Life in 5 Steps*

"Direct, practical, and rich in tools for strengthening the hearts, minds, and souls of men. This book has a depth of wisdom and practicality that is so challenging to achieve. *From the Core* shows the reader exactly how to let the masculine within lead. An instant must read and classic for every man."

Connor Beaton
founder of ManTalks and author of *Men's Work*

FROM THE CORE

A New Masculine Paradigm for Leading with
Love, Living Your Truth, and Healing the World

JOHN WINELAND

sounds true
BOULDER, COLORADO

Sounds True
Boulder, CO 80306

Published 2022

Cover design by Tara DeAngelis
Book design by Karen Polaski

Printed in the United States of America

BK06381

Library of Congress Cataloging-in-Publication Data

Names: Wineland, John (Relationship coach), author.
Title: From the core : a new masculine paradigm for leading with love,
    living your truth, and healing the world / John Wineland.
Description: Boulder, CO : Sounds True, 2022.
Identifiers: LCCN 2021060625 (print) | LCCN 2021060626 (ebook) | ISBN
    9781683649106 (trade paperback) | ISBN 9781683649113 (ebook)
Subjects: LCSH: Men–Identity. | Masculinity. | Self-realization.
Classification: LCC HQ1090 .W585 2022 (print) | LCC HQ1090 (ebook) | DDC
    305.31–dc23/eng/20220204
LC record available at https://lccn.loc.gov/2021060625
LC ebook record available at https://lccn.loc.gov/2021060626

10 9 8 7 6 5 4 3 2 1

TABLE OF CONTENTS

SECTION 8 **LEARNING TO LEAD
AND INTEGRATE YOUR OWN FEMININE**   157

INTRODUCTION

MODERN MEN ARE facing a crisis of masculinity, or so we are told. The recent proliferation of men's work programs, books on deconstructing masculinity, and the post #MeToo discourse calling out the toxic masculine speaks to the swell of interest in the present and future states of men. Despite all of the flack men have received lately (much of it deserved), I see brothers every day who are hungrier than ever to step into their lives more powerfully, who sincerely want to love their partners well, who want to nobly honor, empower, and protect their feminine partners, and who seek to be a source of healing in their communities. Men want to know and experience themselves more powerfully. They want to create lives of real impact and have a purpose beyond simply making money. There are millions who want to stand for justice and to redefine what it means to co-create in their relationships and their world today. So many men want to love from their hearts. The problem as I see it is not in a man's desire to step up, but in his understanding of how to most powerfully do so.

Leading men's groups for almost twenty years now, I have seen these impulses passionately arise with a growing sense of urgency. There is an evolving ethos in more and more men to grow beyond stale tropes of masculinity, to be more vulnerable, and to be more available in the world. But at the same time, I see them struggle with exactly how to embody and manifest these desires at home and in their communities. How can they face the immense pull to numb and to check out, to battle their own demons, negativity, and addictions? So many men still judge their own emotional natures, not knowing how much to reveal or whether their emotionality will be seen as weakness.

A great pain point that men face is the confusion of how to interact with women. Today's woman doesn't need a man to provide or protect her. She can make her own money, she is often more spiritually and emotionally developed, she can parent a child by herself, and she can take care of herself just fine. This fact confuses some men as they attempt to reevaluate and redefine their value propositions as romantic partners. A common complaint I hear is that they are not sure what their feminine partners truly want. Some mistrust the feminine altogether and blame women for their loneliness, as we can see in the rise of involuntarily celibate men. They struggle to fully absorb and navigate this incredibly potent moment of human history with presence, integrity, and love. And yet, I am very clear the vast majority want to.

The paradigm of masculinity we have
inherited no longer works.

These unresolved issues are front and center in so many men who come to my programs and workshops. At the core of most men's exploration into men's work is a desire for belonging. For brotherhood. To love and be loved, and to be seen as noble and good. They wonder what masculinity is and how it can be cultivated as a force of transformative healing; what it means to lead from a healthy, conscious, and unshakeable core; and why the issue of masculinity is even relevant in the world today.

Reclamation

Recent books, podcasts, and published discourses of all sorts have focused on deconstructing masculinity as a whole. I can certainly understand the desire to rid our world of the brutality of patriarchy born of greed and domination, but I think any wholesale inclination to abandon or cancel the masculine principle shows a misunderstanding of what a truly integrated, centered, and grounded masculinity can provide.

Clearly, the paradigm of masculinity we have inherited no longer works. A quick glance at the rising levels of depression, suicide, and addiction among men should make this abundantly clear. We need a new understanding of masculinity and how it can serve, inspire, and support the world—one steeped in the currencies of feeling, integrity, consciousness, presence, and love; one that supports and devotionally celebrates the rise of the Feminine (which I capitalize when referring to the meta-feminine in all of us) in our culture and doesn't try to dominate, control, or capture. We need a framework of practical understanding that embraces the integration of our own tender and emotional sides, without relinquishing our core masculine gifts and most sacred truths. This framework should not simply reward entrepreneurial, technological, or financial successes but seek to reveal and express the more sublime and profound aspects of a man—his core heart, expansive consciousness, and emotional depth. We need a paradigm that clarifies what it means to strengthen, embody, and, when appropriate, lead from a masculinity focused on liberation and born of consciousness and love.

I know that even using the terms *masculine* and *feminine* is controversial. I will take great care throughout this book to suggest that these concepts are energetic gifts every human (and natural phenomenon) possesses, rather than gender-based labels we have been forced to wear. I've placed most of my thoughts on this crucial topic (especially on the subject of my own biases) in the opening of section 1, but for now I simply want to recognize that far too much damage has been caused by a misunderstanding of what constitutes the Masculine (which I capitalize when referring to the meta-masculine in all of us). Unfortunately, we've been taught that it's the same thing as biological maleness, rigidity, stoic strength, domination, and the endless drive for success. The way I learned and conceive of the Masculine has more to do with spaciousness, liberation, and the transmission of consciousness. And so this book is my attempt at reclaiming what it means to *be* masculine and asserting that it is not something men, in particular, should shy away from, but proudly embrace.

The New Masculine Paradigm

From actor Terry Crews taking to social media to assert "vulnerability is not weakness" to hockey star Kurtis Gabriel publicly denouncing homophobia in sports, the list of public figures calling the old guard of masculinity into question continues to grow. Actor and activist Justin Baldoni took to the TED Talks stage to share why he's "Done Being Man Enough" and parlayed that into a book and online presence dedicated to examining the paradigm shift in masculinity and the new role men can play in today's world.

It is abundantly clear that the mainstream culture is beginning to question what type of masculinity should be championed now that the win-at-all-costs machismo of John Wayne and Donald Trump have been so obviously debunked. The patriarchy of old is on its last legs culturally, even if not yet politically and economically. Something new is trying to emerge from the confusion, post-traumatic stress, and cries of yearning for a trustable Masculine from a more vocal and empowered Feminine mainstream.

> *Kill, provide, and conquer* is no longer the
> exemplary expression of who men are.

I believe there is a new paradigm of masculine depth, growth, and leadership starting to poke through that addresses the subtleties needed. Men want to feel more, express more, and be more vulnerable. But they also crave depth—sexually, emotionally, and spiritually—even from other men. They want to be a healing and holding force for the Feminine in their lives. I have seen it, sitting in circles with thousands of men over two decades. Regardless of the form of practice (psychological, meditative, yogic, tantric, recovery, or support group), men crave more clarity, openness, and meticulous responsibility from themselves and each other. The problem is not desire. The problem is that many still don't quite know how.

And yet, no matter how powerful, profound, and impactful the men's work of people like David Deida, Robert Bly, and Sam Keen has been, the overarching framework has failed to do more than spark frothy discussion in small circles of in-group practitioners across the globe. What I am calling for is an approach that elevates the embodied consciousness of men by giving them a structure of practice and growth they can feel immediately and integrate into their daily lives. The cultural landscape is now more ready than ever to support depth, integrity, and feeling. The shifts of awareness have never been greater. Additionally, women have never been more ready to support men's growth. And men are waking up to the understanding that *kill, provide, and conquer*—be it on the battlefield or in the boardroom—is no longer the exemplary expression of who men are.

Men throughout the ages have sought to create physical, emotional, spiritual, and sexual practices in service to love, their world, and the Infinite. What has been missing in the modern cultural definitions of the Masculine is an approach that combines, integrates, and clarifies the disparate calls and approaches to men's work. What I hope to provide in this book is one framework that I have seen thousands of men step into powerfully. There are, of course, myriad other approaches. The paradigm of masculine depth, practice, and leadership I propose takes its cues from numerous streams of thought and practice that have addressed masculine emotional, spiritual, and sexual development throughout the years. Some come directly from the last several decades of men's work, others from Vajrayana Buddhism, various traditions of martial arts, Toltec shamanism, Kundalini Yoga, and the archetypal studies of mytho-poetics. My own experience from teaching embodied men's work has added a thing or two, as well. I hope you'll take what you like and leave the rest. My sincere aspiration is that this set of teachings, offered as humbly and sincerely as I can, will address the fundamental issues facing anyone who is masculine identified today.

What follows is a framework for anyone who wants to cultivate their capacity as an integrated and committed leader. Please understand that these suggestions are never-ending *kriyas*—postures, if you will—that have no conclusive destination. They act as touchstones of reflection and practice meant to be strengthened and explored over time. There is no ultimate arrival, only continual reflection, failure, refinement, and recommitment. With that in mind, this book will invite you to:

1 Take complete responsibility for what has been created in your life and in the world around you by ruthlessly reflecting and refining your relationship to it.

2 Cultivate a presence and awareness that can feel what needs to happen—in all areas of your life—in both the present moment and your current life situation. Then boldly attune to it and take action.

3 Get strong. Not just physically, but by disciplining your awareness and sensitivity, all while strengthening your nervous system to hold and conduct massive amounts of energy.

4 Prioritize grounded depth over comfort in your life. Get highly sensitive to the truth of your heart and the power of your intention.

5 Align with the Feminine in your life by truly understanding what the Feminine—in all forms—wants and needs from you.

6 Become masterful in the art of sexual and energetic polarity. It will empower everything you do in the world in amazing and unsuspected ways.

7 Do the inner work to honor, understand, and express your own Feminine nature. Your capacity to feel and transmit the full expression of your gifts depends on it.

8 Utilize other committed men to discipline yourself to create an impeccable relationship to truth, depth, freedom, and love. Their loving challenge will become one of the enduring gifts of your life.

9 Wake up to the present moment and make it count. Death is coming.

10 Commit to integrating these principles into your life as a never-ending daily practice. True artfulness and creativity will flow from it.

These principles may not fully elucidate all the nuances of being a man in the modern world, but I believe they represent a new paradigm of masculinity that will—if you implement it wholeheartedly—change your life and the lives of those around you.

Three Obstacles

The major problem I see in men is the disconnect between the desire to be a force of consciousness and love in the world, and the actual ability to do so powerfully. At the heart of this disconnect are three primary obstacles. The first is that men have not trained themselves to use mindfulness and meditative practices to go beneath just thinking about their lives and into what would most enhance vitality, clarity, and freedom. The Masculine tends to get caught up in habitual thought loops, trying to answer big questions ("Am I good enough? Will I ever truly succeed? Am I lovable? Am I winning?") rather than cultivating the type of awareness that fosters more life-affirming truths. Being more attached to our thoughts than our bodies only serves to create more disconnection and stress. And it's far too easy for men to get caught up chasing the external trappings of success we've been trained to go after (money, women, intense experiences, etc.) only to find the core truths within us yearning to be cultivated and acknowledged.

Most thoughts we attach to are also driven by fear and insecurity, and our bodies respond to them with more stress hormones than are healthy. In the end, our bodies pay the price with illness, aches, and numbness—while we just keep churning out more self-centered thoughts. This is the reason why meditation teachers throughout time have been trying to get us to detach and witness our thinking rather than attach to it. Thinking might be a natural process, but believing the content of those thoughts as accurate and true is often a problem.

The second obstacle I see men face is a real connection to feeling—not just emotion, but the ability to sense their own bodies and environments. Think of this connection as analogous to the capacity that great martial artists have to feel their space of engagement. They have developed a sixth sense, so to speak—one that allows them to feel out from their physical forms and intuitively know the next move. They don't have to *think* about what to do next; they just sense it and do it.

And finally, the third obstacle is that most men simply lack the skill set needed to affect their environments with conscious awareness and embodied sensitivity. We must be able to fully sense the landscapes we most want to affect before we can access clarity about what needs to happen to create more love, freedom, and expansiveness—be it in romance, a larger community, or work. Additionally, we have to know how to execute. How do you move, lead, and communicate as an embodied expression of consciousness? It can't be said enough that these traits are art forms in the personal, professional, and relational fields that anyone can strengthen and master. They are meant to shift us from the paradigm of acting out of habit and thought rather than enacting with presence and being.

Most men I meet would love to calibrate into this kind of presence and awareness but are not sure how to begin. Do I meditate? Vision quest? Try Kundalini Yoga? CrossFit? Ayahuasca? What does it mean to really feel my life? My lover? My children? And then be a guiding force for them? What does it mean to live fully from the essence of my masculine core?

From the Core

The crisis of masculinity is a crisis of awareness, feeling, and leadership. The answer isn't, as some might suggest, that men shouldn't lead. We need a generation of conscious, embodied men stepping up to offer guidance and direction in their communities, just as we need to support and encourage women to do the same. Men simply need to learn how to engage life from the truest and most profound places within them—their core hearts, their innate stillness, and the wisdom of their conscious awareness.

To do so, we must (re)train ourselves to go into the deepest parts of our bodies, minds, and hearts, moment by moment, and begin to live from there. We need to make decisions from the core, have sex from the core, hug our children from the core, write books from the core, run our companies from the core, and relate to the moment from the core.

Right now, the center of your heart is infinite and still. It is the seed of consciousness. Do you feel it? Right now, there is a space at the bottom of your abdomen that is the power center of your creative energy. Your *dan tien*, as the Taoists would say. Are you breathing fully into it? Right now, there is a channel in the center of your body that extends from your throat to your perineum that is the nexus of your nervous system. Is it open and relaxed? At this moment of your life, your heart is feeling a truth that wants to be expressed. Are you honoring the impulse? All around you, this moment is unfolding perfectly. Can you feel into the center and source of it?

These explorations into your foundational essence and the innate strengths you possess will provide infinite possibilities of love and purpose. They will lead to new understandings about how to live a more fully resourced, profoundly impactful life. All the success in the world won't mean shit if you are underresourced and malnourished in your core.

I will discuss throughout this book how a man can transition from a thought-driven mode of defending and striving into an open, noble, and trustable place of his core heart. I will talk about how to strengthen your nervous system so that you can hold more of what life wants to give you—expanding your window of tolerance through breath, meditation, and intention. And I will invite you to consciously embrace the Warrior in you, not to gain more personal power and dominance over others but as a gift of embodied presence. I will also speak to how you can expand your feeling awareness as a tool of leadership. These practices can shift the trajectory of your life and enhance your magnetism and power. Men need to know this is possible. It's not something we were taught in school or—sadly, for most of us—from our fathers.

We need to understand that conscious leadership—grounded, tethered to the Infinite, and filled with integrity—is a gift. It's a gift that the Feminine and the world craves from us. This texture of masculinity is a presence-centered transmission, not some marketing-driven archetype à la Rambo or the cookie-cutter guys in the *Fast & Furious* franchise. The type of masculinity I'm promoting here liberates, opens, relaxes, and heals. It's about embodying consciousness and freeing love and truth in the moment. It's dedicated to clarity and to serving the greatest good, moment by moment.

There is no end to how far into our true natures we can go. When we do this, everything changes. People around us relax more, even though they may not know why. Our minds clear and sharpen, our hearts soften, and our bodies relax and open. And we can feel it all—what needs to happen next, what needs to be said, and what others require to embody their own relaxation and openness. And that capacity to feel profoundly inward and outward at the same time and then engage from the purest impulse—one that creates the highest freedom and love—is what I define as leadership.

Engaging the World, Prioritizing the Process

This book will guide you into these explorations using a set of principles and practices I have learned and taught for over a decade now. And while I am an unabashed promoter of men's groups (anyone who knows me is familiar with my impossible goal of creating ten thousand men's groups around the world), you certainly don't need one to start engaging yourself, your lover, and the world in the ways I'm describing. The techniques herein will help you release your mind from habitual thoughts, distractions, self-serving strategies, and self-referential worries. They'll also help you expand your awareness and capacity to feel. And instead of disconnecting from the living world on some internal, meditative journey, you'll learn how to relate to your environment and other people while tethered to your core truths. The idea isn't to become more isolated, but to heal, lead, and love others well. To do so, we need to bring the Infinite—merged with the full force of our love—into the world. And if you are willing to spend thirty minutes to an hour in daily practice, your entire approach to love, success, and relationships will change. That's my experience, and an experience I hope to share with as many people as possible.

It's important to say at the onset that my exploration of this work has been inspired and informed by thirteen years of ongoing study and practice in seminars and intensives with renowned spiritual teacher David Deida. His seminal 1997 book, *The Way of the Superior Man*, was my opening soiree into men's work and is still one of the most successful treatises on masculine spiritual development ever written. Deida's many books—along with the thousands of hours I've spent in workshops and trainings—have provided me an invaluable base to build my own approach. For those of you who know Deida's writings, the source material will be obvious. His terminology and framework regarding the nuances, traits, and desires of the Masculine and Feminine in all of us, as well as the art of sexual polarity and his three stages of relationship, are foundational jumping-off points for the work I offer here.

Deida's groundbreaking concepts, such as how the Masculine craves ever more freedom and the Feminine ever more love, what constitutes a masculine and/or feminine essence, and how to deepen in both, as well as how to live into the masculine yoga of sexual polarity, create a backbone for my work here. The language he developed in his extensive oeuvre, found in books like *The Way of the Superior Man*, *Blue Truth*, *Finding God Through Sex*, and *Dear Lover*, have now become commonplace for an entire generation of teachers. It's almost impossible to discuss masculine spiritual development or sexual polarity without drawing from this framework. I will refer to them often in order to unpack how I've employed them as a practitioner and a teacher. My intent is not to simply regurgitate these ideas but to weave them into a metathesis on masculinity and leadership that I see as needed today. They represent my own practice, integration, and (hopefully) some degree of innovation for the modern masculine practitioner. Any mistakes in their presentation are mine.

That being said, my own development along the way hasn't always been pretty. Like many others, I've struggled with my own ego, lack of maturity, and confusion over how to use my personal power as I've grown. I've watched myself and others attempt to develop and lead our relationships only to fall flat because our own reactivity and cultural programming were simply too ingrained. I've seen countless others give up beneath the weight of the emotional stamina and awareness required, and I've nearly given up myself. And I also know well how childhood wounds arise when we dive into yogic and meditative work. It's no wonder that so many people bail after a year or two of practice — it's simply too difficult and too painful. Then again, perhaps we misunderstood what Deida and other teachers were telling us. Perhaps we set the bar too high.

I eventually came to realize that those of us who'd committed ourselves to the path of openness and embodiment were too often focused on the end result, as opposed to the process. Living from your masculine (or feminine) essence is an ongoing journey, no matter your sexual orientation or gender identification. Just as any asana or martial arts practice, embodiment is not meant to be *completed*, but explored and strengthened. There's always more to be discovered — more love, grounding, breath, and awareness. And just like any journey, this work is full of failure, fatigue, detours, recommitments, and recalibrations.

The exercises, concepts, and frameworks I learned along my journey were perpetual openings toward a new way of being, relating, and loving in the world. This is where we as masculine-identified humans tend to get confused. Men's work is a never-ending practice, and the yoga of intimacy is both rewarding and sometimes perilous. For as long as we live, we are constantly in intimacy with the present moment, with the space in which we find ourselves, with the world at large, with the truth of our own hearts, and to all the beings right here with us. So, as has been stated by many before me, the journey is the goal.

The fact that there is no end to the work is often the thing that turns men off, because the Masculine longs for a simple roadmap to all endeavors. It strives for glorious and celebratory completion. Mastery. Checked-off bucket-list experiences. But that's not how it works.

Diving In

If this unfolding exploration and process sounds intriguing, I invite you to take a substantial dive with me in this book. The different sections are meant to be hands-on and practical—how to take full responsibility for your life and relationships, how to make sex an art, how to strengthen your nervous system to stay more present in the face of challenges, how to shepherd and integrate your own feminine gifts and aspects, and, finally, how to relate to death and view it as an ally. All of these sections are meant to give you tools you can apply to your relationship with yourself, your romantic partners, and the world around you.

Your capacity to live from depth—spiritually, physically, emotionally, and sexually—will require you to rework your body-mind habits and rewire your nervous system. The degree of feeling and awareness you'll need will not come easy. These old habits are remnants of our childhood, compounded by years of protective strategy, and they don't typically die without a fight. So there are a few obstacles you're likely to run into as you absorb this work and apply it to your life. I've certainly hit lots of walls on my journey. Remember that almost none of us were taught these concepts, and so they may butt against the grain of what you know to be Masculine or Feminine.

Most of us have developed armor and shielding habits for good reason, but those walls also make it harder to feel into the truths of our core and sense others fully. These habits might not be our fault, but as adults it is our responsibility to recognize our wounds, take care of them, and finally heal. Learning how to enter your core and relax your nervous system will release stuck energy and sometimes pent-up emotions that can rock you, and when that happens, I encourage you to stay with it. Feel it fully. The waves will eventually pass, and you will find yourself with more space and strength than you ever thought possible.

Along the way, you might feel challenged by the level of focus and discipline it takes to go within and stay within. Hell, just focusing on your breath and dealing more directly with your own thoughts for ten minutes can be hard enough. So don't be surprised if it takes a little while for this work to take root. If it were easy to live from the core, everyone would do it constantly. Do your best to weather the discomfort and resist the pull of distracting thoughts, because the presence and awareness you'll develop as a result are more than worth it.

Another common obstacle I hear from men is that they already have too much to do. How are they supposed to learn a whole new set of skills on top of running a business, being a father, and trying to be a good partner? Well, that's up to you, and I certainly can't tell you how to prioritize your life. But I know what it's like to fall into the habit of prioritizing the wrong things. And I also know the power of shifting those priorities to endeavors that foster the most positive impact. Believe me: if you develop the discipline to go within first, while grounding into your true nature, your life will change and in ways you never expected. It's natural to experience resistance when you start living from the core, but that resistance is just a part of the process—just one thing among many that comes with the path.

When you hit your edge, relax as much as you can. Take it easy. Nuzzle up to your edge rather than trying to blast through it all the time. It's like a good stretch: you breathe, relax, and stay with the discomfort until it gives a little. You don't just rip open your hamstring. But neither do you back off entirely. You stick with it.

Over time, your growth will be exponential, and your relationship to discomfort will change. That being said, the Masculine grows in discomfort, challenge, and discipline. So, as we head into this exploration of core masculine principles and practices, face your resistance and question it, but do so consciously. You may just find that a whole new set of opportunities is available to you—a way of living that will change the whole trajectory of your life.

THE INTEGRATED MASCULINE

The Masculine and Feminine in Everyone

The Mystic Law, the Infinite, the Present Moment—in nature, in the cosmos, in any human—has a latent and manifest aspect. An essence that is constant and unchanging and a manifest expression that is never the same twice. These polarities exist in all phenomena and are what we call the Masculine and the Feminine.

It's important to clarify these terms as they relate to the framework I have adopted. I also want to tease apart the traditional concepts of the Masculine from *male-only* and the Feminine from *female-only*. Instead, they are polar representations in natural phenomena that manifest in all humans, regardless of sexual orientation or gender identification. They have also been an essential component of spiritual traditions for thousands of years: yin/yang, Shiva/Shakti, alpha/omega, consciousness/energy, and so on. As with my favored terms (Masculine and Feminine), these are all just labels people have used to speak about the ineffable polarities of the universe, and ancient traditions have long understood the value of honoring and working with them as a means of fostering health, balance, and wholeness. It's only been in the past few hundred years that the concepts of *masculine* and *feminine* became co-opted in service of male-driven power structures, consumption economies, and systemic social inequities, rather than a framework that could be used to understand the wonderful complexities of human relationships and the cosmos itself.

If the words *masculine* and *feminine* have too much charge for you (which would be understandable), I hope you'll consider substituting other terms that Deida has used to unpack this polarity: structure and flow, awareness and energy, fullness and emptiness, or whatever other set of polarities work for you. The point is not the terms but their energetic signatures. There are centuries of gender-related baggage connected to these terms, to be certain, but my intention in using them is to reclaim and reintegrate universal concepts to foster a clearer expression of our relational and sexual natures while also providing you new lenses to understand the different and often challenging parts of ourselves. Regardless of gender and label, these energies manifest and move in every human, in every moment, in every corner of the universe.

What we call them is less important than the experiential understanding of how consciousness and love are trying to move through us in endlessly profound and evolving ways.

It's time to wrestle the limited concepts of masculinity and femininity from the patriarchy that created them.

As David Deida explains, the Masculine is the part of us that does not change. It is the essential core of consciousness itself—the part of us that will always just *be*. It is the witness aspect described in numerous spiritual traditions as simply *aware*—the part of you that is registering this thought and is aware of having it right now. It is the essential *you*—the you before you had a name. It is the empty space that some say inhabits the core of every atom and holds all elements of the universe together. It is the infinite moment stretching out to the end of the cosmos, the rock that holds and guides the flow of the waterfall. It is the quiet totality of death that all natural phenomena return to, eventually giving way to new life. It is the dissolution into complete rest during the most pristine Savasana—the final pose in most yoga practices.

The part of you that is drawn to these aspects of existence is your Masculine. It's the part of you that craves peace, wants all things to end, and is completely at bliss in infinite silence. Your capacity to access, animate, and express this unchanging core of you through the body is the essence of masculine practice. This is what I mean by *masculine embodiment*. However, this is only half of who you are.

The Feminine in every moment and every human is the constantly flowing and changing nature of all existence. It's the energy that inexplicably makes your heart beat and your blood flow. It's the part of you that feels everything—your sensitivity, your thoughts, and emotions that emerge and then recede. It is life's constant unfolding—the thought that wants to manifest as creation, the emotion that calls to be felt, your five senses, your sexual hunger, your desire to create your life's mission. The Feminine is everything happening within and without you, in each successive moment. And the part of you drawn to feeling, expressing, and flowing in these facets of existence is the embodiment of the Feminine.

These are the polarities present in all aspects of cosmic and natural existence, and all of us have both fully available within us at any moment.

It's time to wrestle the limited concepts of masculinity and femininity from the patriarchy that created them and reclaim them as sacred aspects of our humanity that we can develop and strengthen with intention and practice. They are our innate, divinely given fountainheads of creativity, sexuality, leadership, and freedom. When we consciously expand both, we become integrated and whole and more available to the world. From this space, our greatest gifts emerge.

The Masculine, Nonbinary and Same-Sex Relating

As I will say repeatedly, these traits and energetic capacities live in all of us. The whole point of this book is to help anyone who desires to step deeper into a more conscious practice of masculine leadership and spiritual practice, as well as add tools and approaches that have immediate impact in their relationships, be they a cisgender man who identifies primarily as masculine, a woman in a same-sex relationship who prefers to lead, or a nonbinary person simply wanting to stretch their masculine capacities as I describe them here. Humans are infinitely beautiful and complex, and there are countless other possibilities of personal and relational expression. The recognition of the Masculine and Feminine within us is meant to empower us with practical tools as opposed to confine us to stale tropes.

People regularly ask me how this work applies to same-sex relating or LGBTQ issues of identity. My admittedly biased answer is that these concepts and practices apply to everyone. From my perspective, the Masculine and Feminine are universal attributes, although I understand that describing their natures is fraught with difficulty, much of which — due to my own preferences and stations — I have trouble recognizing. Because I am a white, heterosexual, cisgender, masculine-identified man, my biases, both known and unknown, are inseparable from my specific life journey.

When I use the term *feminine*, I am most often talking about feminine-identified humans (most often, but not always, women) as well as the Feminine within those who identify as male. My use of *masculine*, in turn, primarily refers to masculine-identified people, in addition to the Masculine aspects of people who identify as female. I realize this frame is not as inclusive as I'd like it to be. In my work, I mostly interact with cisgender heterosexual men and women—the great majority of whom identify as primarily masculine or feminine in their nature and desires—and so this book is written primarily with my experiences and theirs in mind. That being said, I have seen over and over that the concepts here can be applied to all humans and their relationships, no matter how they manifest.

You've probably already noticed that I rely heavily on the terms *men* and *women*, as well as their associated pronouns. You'll also find words like *human, person, partner, they, them*, and so on, as well as some examples to drive home my belief that this work is for everybody, regardless of how they identify. In the process, I have no doubt that I'll fall short of being able to speak to everyone, and I ask your forgiveness at the onset. If you have an interest in the energetics of sexual polarity, I hope you'll see past the limitations of my language and find something beneficial for you and the people you relate with.

The Masculine-Feminine Continuum

So, to further unpack this presentation of the polarity, I invite you to imagine a spectrum of being with extreme Masculine on one end and fully Feminine on the other. In this presentation, that means stillness, emptiness, and the infinite expanse of consciousness on one end of the spectrum, and love, luminescence, and the continual flow of energy on the other. We can see these polarities at play in the natural world on the tiniest and unimaginably giant scales. Consider the grandest mountain or an expansive desert: motionless, solid, wide, and immovable. Then, as we move farther and farther away from stillness, the spectrum starts to range into the movement and energetic transmission of the Feminine—storm clouds, waves, wind through the trees.

As humans, we are expressions and mirrors of the natural world. From this vantage, it is easy to see that someone standing as grounded depth and presence could be felt as more "masculine" than one dancing ecstatically. It is simply because they are reflecting the Masculine principles of nature through the body. Or how a man moving or speaking with slow and steady cadence would have a more nourishing impact on the feminine nervous system than one speaking in a staccato and high-pitched manner. And so, as masculine beings it is important to know that if we want to bring a relaxing and trustable presence to any moment, slowing down and grounding is paramount. In this way, we can impact any situation, person, or environment with the transmission of grounded strength and consciousness. From here, we can feel an emotion deeply. We can have profound sex. We can communicate or hear a difficult truth. Through our breath, posture, attention, and openness, we become the structure and witness, both receiving and observing the moment. This is the texture of masculine practice that the Feminine humans I hear from daily are craving.

For anyone endeavoring to expand their capacity and range along this continuum, the first step should be to recognize where they naturally fall. That being said, value judgments about being "too feminine" or "too masculine" are a waste of time. What does matter is that you are aware of your baseline along the spectrum I described above. Don't worry if sizing yourself up takes some time, as you are learning about the internal workings of your psycho-emotional body—not to mention your own heart. It took me a couple of years of personal reflection, asking my men's group and mentors, and questioning what I am most drawn to or triggered by. The more I learned about the nuances of masculine and feminine energetics and tendencies, the more I came to see I lean slightly more toward the feminine side.

I'm not alone. There are many men who have energetic, responsive, and emotional bodies. Coming to this realization about myself required a bit of ego relaxation and compassionate reflection. I am passionate and often fiery. I am also intuitive, loving, and sensitive to my environment. I prefer community, family, and consensus building to a single-minded, solitude-driven, purpose-at-all-costs type of living. That's simply the nature and impulse of the emotional body I received in this lifetime.

The ability to ground and become still was never taught to me, and so my nervous system needed to learn how to do so later in my life. Essentially, I had to install more masculine capacity into my body through dedicated practice. It took a few years, but I discovered the core place beneath my emotional body and nervous system that was deep and peaceful, although my emotional body remained primarily feminine. So, too, was my mind, which tended to jump from thought to thought rather than lock in on one at a time. But my physical body, spiritual body, and sexual body skewed very clearly masculine. These aspects of my being now work in harmony most of the time. I can bring awareness, stillness, and structure to my fire, as well as my vulnerabilities, and it now has a positive effect on me and others.

Other men I have seen come to this work with much less reactive, stiller, often denser physical and emotional bodies. They may feel more at home in solitude than in feeling or intimate relating. Often they are more stoic and focused on outcomes but less attached to energetic sensitivities or the expression of emotion. Men like this will often find their feminine partners are hurt by a lack of emotional availability or sensitivity, and that their work may lean toward fostering their capacities for sensitivity, feeling, and expression. If you slot into this category, you might not have been taught how to feel emotions and move energy, but you can cultivate these skill sets with some of the practices outlined later in this book.

> The integrated Masculine draws from
> an arsenal of true wholeness.

No matter how much capacity and range you develop along the Masculine/Feminine continuum, your baseline will not fundamentally change. Coming to peace with that home point and understanding your natural set of needs and limitations is incredibly helpful and freeing. Where you want to develop from there is completely your choice— coming from a clear understanding of your innate tendencies and a conscious decision to expand in whatever direction your heart and the world are calling you. For now, just know there is nothing wrong with where you are in this moment. Your body-mind is nuanced and uniquely you. Whatever your home base on this spectrum, you can expand infinitely in either direction. If you are denser and more Masculine, know that you can cultivate immense amounts of feeling and sensation as new paints in your palette. If you are more comfortable in flow and emotional expression, grounding and tethering to consciousness is simply a matter of practice. There is so much more of you available to give than you know.

The Integrated Masculine

The new paradigm of masculine leadership and co-creation I advocate is the cultivation and integration of each person's fully expressed and embodied Masculine, thoughtfully and consciously united with their internal Feminine. What this actually looks like will vary from person to person, from moment to moment. The best way to think about this union is as the conscious awareness and immense capacity to feel and express what is most true in any moment. And then to create powerful action from stillness, intuit what is needed from a strong tether to consciousness, and then act upon that intuition to create the greatest liberation of love and freedom. This ability to feel through the body-mind to what is alive in the field—be it a relationship, family, business, or a movement—while feeling the world completely, is the most valuable form of presence anyone can practice. Deciding what is needed to create the greatest openness, freedom, and love from that awareness is what I would call powerful masculine leadership.

In my experience, there's a growing desire to redefine the concept of masculinity from the hard driven, win-at-all-cost archetypes of the twentieth century into a more conscious, loving, and noble transmission of depth, presence, and integrity. This new paradigm of masculinity does not deny our primal natures but harnesses them consciously in service of love and freedom. This requires not just a strengthening of a man's nervous system but an enabling of his ability to integrate the fullness of his grounded, clear consciousness and boundless capacity to feel sensation and transmit love—in addition to experiencing and expressing whatever emotional truths are moving through him.

The goal isn't just to become tougher or stronger, nor is it about turning so completely to the meditative realms that you observe the outside world in a detached fashion. It's also not a call to be so vulnerable and attached to your feelings that you lose all grounding and awareness of your present reality. The integrated Masculine draws from an arsenal of true wholeness—a strong body-mind and heart, tethered to the Infinite, and always sensitive to what's needed in every moment.

Why hasn't this way of being already evolved? The short answer is that most of the world is still attempting to free itself from the grip of the patriarchal—and far too often toxic—values of conquest and domination. Over the past few thousand years, we went from primarily dominating nature, to dominating other humans, to dominating business, to dominating technology. Sensitivity, empathy, and the ability to feel the ripple effects of one's actions or states of being were not necessarily celebrated traits. Scan the histories of virtually any country. With the exception of a few matriarchies throughout the millennia, you will find stories of domination and oppression everywhere, almost exclusively at the hands of men. These principles of masculinity still run resolutely through the collective psyche. What has been celebrated and what most men still internalize as masculine value stems from the collective psychosocial definition of masculinity—distorted and amplified by the entertainment and marketing industries of the previous century.

And while the 1960s and 1970s gave men permission to celebrate the primarily feminine values of peace, love, and personal expression—giving rise to generations of men who identify much more honestly with their feelings, needs, and desires—it was mostly enacted as a reaction against male-dominated authority, rather than a conscious movement of unification and integration. ·

If we zoom out, we see the unintegrated Masculine in virtually every arena of human suffering. Shattered families, endless warring, social and economic inequality, and climate disruption all stem from it. And while *From the Core* is not meant to be a treatise on the toxic history of the patriarchy, I make this point for two key reasons.

First, we are at an unprecedented time in history where modalities of spiritual, yogic, and meditative practices have merged with a technological explosion to make the unification I present here available for anyone who wants it. Second, it has become increasingly difficult for us to convince ourselves that we can separate the micro from the macro. Pathologies of distorted masculinity take hold first as unexpressed or unexperienced feelings, unconscious impulses of control and domination, unowned and unhealthy sexuality, and unacknowledged judgment of ourselves and others. For this reason, our most essential work must take place at home—in our own cores, romantic relationships, families, and communities. These are the most fruitful places to cultivate healthier, holistic, and more integrated forms of masculine leadership.

This lack of true understanding of what a whole and integrated Masculinity might look like has perpetuated cultural, sociopolitical, and personal conflict. Less discussed, but even more important, are the similar conflicts occurring within many a man's internal landscape: "What do I do with my feelings? How can I show strength without being a macho asshole? How do I own my primal sexuality without being predatory? How can I heal from my addictions and harmful habits without becoming uber rigid?"

I have watched men struggle with these questions and others for years now. Far too many of them either reject their wilder emotional nature or fail to create enough structure, discipline, integrity, and depth in their daily lives. Most of the time they have no awareness that they are doing so; it simply shows up as collapse, dysfunction, or dissatisfaction— particularly in their relationships. And even if they are aware of this lack of integrated harmony, most have not been given the framework to understand and express the polarities of emotional truth and integral awareness through their unique body-minds.

For example, a man (or anyone, for that matter) may have been raised to deny his highly sensitive and emotional nature in favor of a linear path to success and satisfaction. He may have been rewarded with love and praise for victory and achievement, but not for his emotional tenderness. Maybe he learned to judge his more vulnerable needs or insecurities as inconvenient or weak. Perhaps, as a protective mechanism to survive, he developed a layer of armor that limited his ability to feel both himself and others. Maybe he saw his jealousy, desire, and yearning for love as shameful, burying all of it under a facade of bravado or achievement. Maybe he compensated for his fears and insecurities with material success, stoicism, or physical prowess. In my experience, most men rely on some combination of these strategies.

No true change in behavior or thinking
can come without an awakened body, an
activated heart, and a spacious mind.

In some men, this is easy to spot; in others, it's quite subtle. I actually see it play out in people of all sorts, from world-class athletes to successful CEOs. They're often unaware of their more hidden and difficult feelings, and they may judge themselves or numb the discomfort with distraction rather than sit in the fire of their deeper truths and needs. They do not know these more challenging feelings are portals to a transformative capacity of relating and inner strength. They will often see them as something to overcome rather than the gifts they are.

It's not completely their fault, of course. Most men are the inheritors of a cultural epigenetics that didn't teach them to feel with depth and integrity, and technology has seen to it that distraction and instant numbness and shallow gratification are constantly at hand. That's precisely why I emphasize conscious awareness and physical relaxation to access and integrate our feeling natures.

I will offer some specific practices for you to train yourself into this depth of awareness and feeling without losing any of your strength, drive, or passion. The unifying factor in all of these practices is your body. No true change in behavior or thinking can come without an awakened body, an activated heart, and a spacious mind.

On the other end of the spectrum, men may have been habitually taught to deny their more ruthless, primal natures and are instead encouraged to cultivate heightened sensitivity and feeling. The men of my generation and the one that followed learned to acknowledge feelings and to express their thoughts and emotions with much more ease. This is good. And healthy! Many, like myself, were raised by single mothers and internalized their mother's feminine. The pendulum swing that occurred in the 1960s and 1970s was as overdue as the feminist movements of the same time. However, just as some women today are realizing they were taught to overemphasize their masculine capacities to the point of imbalance, some men are just now coming to understand the polar truth for themselves.

Many masculine-identified people I encounter have not developed the nervous system strength, body-mind integrity, or pliable awareness to stay conscious, open, and energetically grounded in the midst of potent feelings. Or they may celebrate their awareness of thoughts and emotions to the point of indulgence, often losing sight of what the present moment requires in terms of leadership or clarity. They may be hyperattached to self-centered emotionality, placing their awareness so fully on "what they are noticing" about their own fears and insecurities that they become incapable of noticing the feelings and needs of others. Neither of these polarities presents the whole man. And while most of us fall somewhere in the middle of the two extremes just described, almost all of us skew to one edge of the spectrum or the other.

If neither stoic, hard-driving toughness nor stereotypical New Age sensitivity reveals the true possibilities of masculine fullness, then what does? We are at the precipice of a new, more complete "wholearchy" that celebrates a man's physical and mental integrity as well as his ability to feel others and the world with exquisite sensitivity. This is, I believe, the Third Stage man Deida describes in many of his teachings. The problem I have seen over and over is that few are willing to take on the disciplines required to cultivate this kind of completeness.

Be it someone as polished and educated as Dr. Martin Luther King Jr. or as raw and vibrant as Greta Thunberg, one common trait among all inspiring leaders is they elevate others with a combination of clear awareness, fierce passion, and unwavering devotion to a cause greater than mundane success, accolades, and comfort. They have naturally integrated consciousness, passion, and love while pressing it into the world as a gift that is uniquely theirs.

What I hope to lay out here is a path to awaken the same in you so that you can offer it into the world—offer it through your lovemaking, parenting, friendship, and work. Not to just give it, but to liberate those around you with it. If you listen closely, you will understand that this is exactly what other men, women, and the world have been craving from you.

The Conscious Warrior in You

Found in mythologies around the world, the Warrior is revered for skill, bravery, nobility, and honor. It's the part of us willing to fight, kill, and die to protect the people we love or a cause we truly believe in. It is the embodiment of fierce devotion. Although the entertainment and video gaming industries have distorted the Warrior into a mere killing machine, the archetype still speaks powerfully to our enduring need to devote ourselves to others. Think of any blockbuster movie or popular television series, and you'll almost always find the Warrior fighting to liberate humanity (or at least some small portion of it) from dire threat. It's the Warrior who ultimately shields us from annihilation and evil.

Both men and women stand to benefit from passionately and artfully integrating the Warrior archetype into their lives. Martial artists and spiritual masters throughout the ages have encouraged us to see past the violence and wrathful actions typically associated with warriorhood and realize that at their core Warriors are embodiments of courage, consciousness, and love. The Buddhist teacher Chogyam Trungpa was known for his unique interpretation of warriorhood, which he defined as facing one's fears and vulnerabilities with bravery and unconditional friendliness. Carlos Castaneda described the Warrior's training in terms of meticulous integrity, ruthless self-reflection, and consciousness.

Warrior energy can feel uncomfortable and dangerous.

All of the traits that have made the Warrior so impactful throughout history—bravery, dedication, sacrifice, and honor—can be learned, practiced, and transmitted through the body at any moment—in service of love, truth, and freedom. Most of us will never need to fight in wars for the liberation of humanity, but we can regularly fight against closed-heartedness, selfishness, and delusion. And we can bravely make a stand for compassion and heightened awareness. We can practice more fierceness and vulnerability with our own hearts and those of others.

Mahatma Gandhi was a conscious Warrior, as was Rosa Parks. Both bravely dedicated their lives in service of justice and freedom. A more current example is Ken Nwadike Jr., who runs the Free Hugs Project (you may have seen his videos on Facebook or YouTube). Nwadike, a Black man, uses hugs and dialogue to build bridges among white supremacists, law enforcement officers, and Black communities, and he and his team regularly brave almost exclusively white rallies to make connections with men and women on the front lines of the "opposition." The Free Hugs Project regularly offers friendship and dialogue to men carrying Confederate flags. There are often heated discussions involved, and Nwadike often has to hold his ground and express his humanity and dignity. But his willingness to stay connected and keep his heart available almost inevitably results in smiles, hugs, and lasting shifts in the people he engages. This is the kind of warriorhood that is possible if we train our nervous systems and utilize the immense energy of our hearts.

Some men eschew Warrior energy at all costs, citing the damage it has done, and some of that hesitancy and avoidance is understandable. But it's also true that many of us have been trained to be polite and passive at all costs (what author and teacher Robert Glover has called the Nice Guy Syndrome, and what Deida refers to as the 50/50 stage of Masculine development), so Warrior energy can feel uncomfortable and dangerous. This was the case with me, as well as with other men I know who grew up without a strong father figure. Later in life, I learned to access and cultivate these energetic capacities—bringing equal parts Warrior and Lover through my navel and heart until others could feel the integration of the two in my nervous system. I undertook this in men's work because other men could feel that I was holding back an important texture of my love to the world, and they challenged me to become more available. Charming and disarming only took me so far; I also had to find my sharpness—and my core strength. I had to learn what it meant to be fiercely committed to the transmission of love.

PRACTICE AWAKENING THE WARRIOR IN YOUR LIFE

What are you willing to die for? What values do you have that deserve the devoted commitment of the Warrior in you? What calls out for your relentless compassion and fierce love? Perhaps your friend is taking his spouse for granted and needs to pull his head out of his ass, or maybe your kids are addicted to their digital devices.

Is someone in your business unethical or abusive? Or maybe it's time for you to step up for a greater cause—climate change, for example, or social inequality. Where can you bravely wield the sword of truth for the sake of making the world a better place? Are you stuck in some self-indulgent loop that requires you to get fierce with yourself? Be relentless in your exploration. Choose one person or area where you will bring your passion, and apply the fierce love and courage of your Warrior there.

Masculinity as a Transmission

At its core, masculinity is simply an embodied transmission of grounded consciousness, stillness, integrity, and clarity—through a human body. Just as femininity can be said to be the transmission of love, energy, pleasure, and flow. Gender and sexual orientation matter not. What matters is the capacity to express certain traits through our physical, emotional, and energetic bodies. These are moment-to-moment embodied yogas to be practiced, not permanent states to be attained.

As Deida explains, the foundational Masculine spiritual practice throughout the ages has been to touch, rest, and open the most unchanging place within our awareness. Zen and Vipassana meditation are examples of this kind of witness-based awareness practice meditation, and they are incredibly blissful and freeing for the Masculine in any human. Unfortunately, these practices can sometimes lack the radiant aspect that transforms meditators from mere observers of phenomena to full-bodied transmitters of that phenomena. Your capacity to share your inner realization through an embodied transmission *is* the purest form of masculinity. This is the difference between being aware of the Infinite versus pressing infinite consciousness and feeling through your physical presence in a way that moves and relaxes those around you.

Any feminine practitioner could do this as well. I have had women stand at the front of the room in workshops and demonstrate the masculine transmission through their bodies, while their partners practice flowing and opening as love. It is powerful to see the energetics play out similarly, even when traditional gender roles are reversed.

Rarely do we tease apart the difference
between transmitting masculinity and
doing so-called masculine stuff.

Our male-dominated society feeds men's insatiable desire for more — more wealth, more sex, more power. This historical impulse that men have foisted on the world is part of what is nowadays referred to as the *toxic masculine*. True masculinity, in comparison, doesn't need anything. Its nature is freedom, not conquest. It occurs as love, not dominance. Its transmission is a gift, not a show of strength.

There has been much confusion over the past few years as to what defines masculinity, and rightfully so. We have been culturally bludgeoned with ad-driven imagery of what makes a man masculine, and centuries of war and domination have entrenched in our collective psyche a stream of brutally heroic images meant to convey what a man is supposed to be — or, more precisely, what a man *does*. Primarily, these images have been about "winning" at whatever a man is doing — chopping wood, parenting a child, waging war, scoring a touchdown, climbing a mountain, or seducing a lover. More recent discussions of masculinity include sharing his vulnerable side or following the strong women in his life, as people continue to try to break free of patriarchal iconography. But rarely do we tease apart the difference between transmitting masculinity and doing so-called masculine stuff. We just assume the capacities of strength, insight, and seduction a man uses to do these things must be his masculinity, when in reality there's quite a difference.

Deida often uses "the Masculine" to mean the effortless, ever-present consciousness of body, mind, and all experience. Masculinity, as I define it, is the result of resting in a state of depth while tethered to an embodied consciousness that is infinite and immutable. It's also transmitting that sacred and timeless connection in our movements, decisions, and ways of being in the world. In this way, our activities become offerings to create freedom and clarify others. It is an entirely different way of being rather than doing.

Of course, accessing this level of depth and openness through the human body (especially the male body) takes work. It requires physical practice to allow breath to quiet our minds, wake up our feeling bodies, and calm our hyperaroused and often overloaded nervous systems. As you do this, your connection to the flow of life force (known in some circles as *chi* or *prana*) will strengthen, and you will be able to access a deeper space within. Your body-mind will align with the force that drives all phenomena, and you will begin to naturally radiate it into your environment. You will feel and be felt as a stronger, more grounded, conscious presence. This is a key piece of the revolutionary integration I have been discussing.

Accessing this depth of feeling also requires opening ourselves to that which we often do not want to experience or feel. And doing so with an activated heart. With the exception of some First Nation tribes who teach young warriors to hunt with open-hearted reverence and feeling, most men throughout the centuries trained themselves to fight, hunt, and kill with remote efficiency. This armoring has been required over thousands of years for men to feed and protect themselves and their families, despite the fact that, for most of us, such an approach today is either outmoded or no longer necessary.

In the past fifty years or so, men have come around to acknowledging the value in *feeling*. Even so, the effort can prove difficult for some of us. This book will suggest how to make body-mind and heart awareness a rewarding and powerful habit and will also help you access more life force and strengthen your nervous system to do what needs to be done in your world, whether that takes the form of making a stand for a brother in trouble, ravishing your lover, or artfully guiding the lives of your children or community. Mastering this skill set will empower you to lead yourself and those around you with more vitality and grounded presence. You will be more trustable and stable. You will be a more effective and magnetic leader. What I refer to as masculine leadership is the set of actions and decisions you make when you are securely rooted in the space of activated life force and rested consciousness.

This new paradigm of masculinity calls for us to be rooted in conscious awareness and unflinching responsibility of how our state of being affects those around us. It invites us to feel intensely, disavow numbness, and turn away from the win-at-all-costs dogma that has driven men for far too long. It empowers us to develop the capacity to hold more sensation and energy in our bodies, which will in turn provide us with heightened emotional intelligence. From this place, we become as attuned to what life wants to move through us as we are to what we want. What will best serve love? What will make the greatest art? What do those around us need?

It requires feeling beyond childhood wounds and programming and into an understanding of true service. Making decisions from an embodied and integrated place also requires a level of depth and awareness few men have wanted to cultivate—save for monks, yogis, and certain types of devout practitioners of martial arts throughout the centuries. The great irony I have seen in my life and the lives of men around me is that this way of living becomes an incredibly powerful strategy for all-around success, as the people around us become inspired by our feeling awareness, grounded presence, and integrity. They want to be near us. The Feminine and the world trust us more. Others invite us to lead and are willing to pay us more, because they can feel all that we have cultivated within.

This form of sacred and integrated masculine leadership is, of course, a lifelong discipline that falls squarely into the "simple, but not easy" category of humanistic and spiritual practice. But if you are inspired to lead yourself, your love, and the world at this crucial moment of history, it is the only place to set the bar.

PRACTICE INSPIRED IMPULSE

Sit quietly in a comfortable space for ten minutes and relax your breath. Let all thought go as much as you can and try to feel your life. Don't think about it—*feel* it. Become aware of the field of existence you know as your life—your family, work, relationships, and so on. From a place of quiet, deep feeling, let what needs to happen emerge as an inspired impulse rather than a strategy. What needs to be added or removed in your life? What calls to be enhanced? Notice how you feel when you imagine things moving in these directions. Do you become more relaxed, excited, or inspired? Write down one or two concrete outcomes that need to happen to serve the quality, clarity, and integrity of your life. I recommend relying on this practice at least once a week.

LEADERSHIP AND RESPONSIBILITY

The Art of Integrated Masculine Leadership

All the money, freedom, toys, or sex we enjoy temporarily—even the contributions we make to our communities—don't truly scratch the itch of real soul satisfaction. The Masculine loves to think in absolutes and in terms of the single-minded focus of achievement, but the true transmission of our value emerges in relationship—not completion or accumulation. Imagine a great waterfall, a two-hundred-foot-tall redwood, a martial artist, or a particularly moving poem or painting. What each of these has in common is a unique synthesis of structure and flow, consciousness and expression, stillness and movement. The giant tree is seemingly still, yet massive amounts of life force are flowing through the trunk and roots, feeding and being fed by the sunlight through the leaves, moving downward, outward, and up continuously. The massive waterfall is formed by an ancient mountain and rock guiding the powerful flow of water—which in turn slowly reshapes the rock over centuries. The martial artist moves from stillness but constantly feels, reacts, and then returns again to stillness, before feeling the next move. The poem or painting is consciousness held by a structure, beautifully expressed through words, color, form, and energy.

Most everyone understands these concepts intellectually, but we often don't recognize that our relationships are like this, too. A moment of profound relational leadership is artful, whether it's Prince blasting open a concert hall with his energy and presence, a president inspiring the nation with a passionate speech, or you knowing exactly what your romantic partner needs in lovemaking tonight. All are works of art, born of immaculate awareness and deep feeling.

And what makes a great artist? Hours and hours of practicing, honing, and refining their skills. A surgeon, a musician, and an accountant all operate within different settings, but they all bring some level of artistry to the thousands of hours they dedicate to improving their skills. You can apply this same commitment to broaden your capacity to transmit love, depth, and presence to your everyday life. It is simply a skill set most men were not taught to revere, nor were they taught to understand the dynamics of what creates transformative trust and the capacity to stir the hearts of our lovers and the world through our way of being.

The transmission of masculine leadership is an art that conveys relaxation over striving, feeling over focus. It prioritizes being full-body slotted into the present moment versus attached to some distracted thought, future project, or fantasy. Those whom we endeavor to lead in the world — be it in love, work, or service — need us to develop the artistry of depth, feeling, and expression that creates real impact. Real inspiration.

Cultivate the Sensitivity and Structure to Lead Any Moment

First, let's clarify what I mean by *sensitivity*. I'm not talking about the emotional fragility that's too often misconstrued for that term. I mean the combination of awareness and feeling that any human can cultivate to experience the texture of themselves and another or an environment at profound levels. From that experience, actions often emerge organically. There is very little thought involved, if any. Think of a skilled hunter who has spent countless hours in the stillness of nature, attuning their body to the forest. They have developed immaculate sensitivity to even the most subtle changes in temperature or wind direction. They react from that sensitivity, not from strategy. Or call to mind a martial artist who has trained so completely that they can sense the slightest muscle twitch or energetic impulse from an opponent and strike automatically, without thought.

The same kind of immaculate attunement is possible in our own awareness and relationships. How does one start to cultivate an immaculately sensitive body-mind? It becomes the result of training your body, heart, mind, and nervous system to feel yourself and everything around you. Once this is mastered, you can expand to feel the space you are in. If you place your awareness on the breath of your partner and relax, you become more sensitive to their nervous system. This will have remarkable impacts on your sex life and your intimacy (more on that later). If you focus in the same way on your heart and spine, you become more sensitive to what is true in your body. Contemplative arts like qigong and tai chi are known for sharpening this kind of sensitivity, but all you really need to start is enhanced breathing, more focused awareness, and relaxation.

PRACTICE ENHANCED BREATHING

Begin in a seated, relaxed position. Place your awareness on bringing your breath into your lower abdomen, expanding the belly on the inhale and allowing it to fall inward on the exhale. Focus your mind on simply following the breath. Relax your shoulders, jaw, and chest. Bring all of your body-mind awareness to your expanding belly. Feel your diaphragm and pelvic floor move. Sense your organs as they receive more oxygen. Now do the same for your genitals, noticing the blood flow and sensitivity begin to shift. Feel your abdomen expand gently in all directions. Spend three minutes engaged in this practice and explore the following: In what ways are you more sensitive to your body? To your motions and sensations? The space around you? Done daily or multiple times a day, your body-mind will become better able to sense the micro fluctuations of energy and emotion around you. Your body, rather than just your mind, becomes more open and available to the information of the moment. Now you are much more prepared to lead yourself and those around you with relaxed depth and sensitivity.

From this place, what can you feel that you most need to notice and attend to? Maybe you can feel that your spouse is stressed out? Or that your children are in pain that they're trying to hide? Maybe there's incredible love and joy in your home that you might otherwise miss? No matter the truth of the moment, if you engage in this practice, you will become more receptive and relaxed to influence your internal and external environment.

This relaxed capacity is only part of the masculine gift of leadership. The second—and equally important—part of leading a moment will often require structure born from your heightened feeling awareness. If you can feel that your spouse is indeed stressed, what could you offer that would help her relax back into the loving, radiant human you know her to be? Does she need physical attention? A bath, a glass of wine, or a full-bodied kiss? Some time alone to herself? A conversation to clear the residue of her day? Notice how your attention from this place impacts her and adjust as needed. This might mean becoming more playful, directive, or even hands-off. But trust your impulse, as it has arisen through your powerful practice.

> Presence, sensitivity, groundedness, breath,
> and awareness are the building blocks for
> mastery in virtually any endeavor.

You can similarly tune in to the field of your business—for example, your clients or coworkers. What do they need? How can their needs be addressed powerfully rather than habitually? Feel it rather than think about it. The moment you create direction and structure (a plan, even a spontaneous one) from the depth of your feeling awareness, you are now creating from a deeper place in you, rather than your often habitual and outcome-driven thinking. This is how a culture of leadership directed by sensitivity is built. One attentive moment at a time. Don't worry about missteps. They will come. But over time, your intuition will strengthen, and you will know what will actually liberate and relax those around you in some way.

Nowhere have I seen this more than in my moments of teaching. I lead groups of people through exercises filled with emotional, sexual, and psychic energy. Whatever plan I had ten minutes in the past is useless when the whole field changes, which it usually does. I regularly have to stop, ground, connect to the current field of energy and the core consciousness beneath it, and then use the sensitivity I have cultivated over the years to feel where the group needs to go. I am often amazed at how, once plugged in to both grounded consciousness and the texture of the room, the appropriate language and direction just emerge. There's not a lot of thinking involved, but there is a form of knowing.

The great lie we have told ourselves is that art and mastery exist only in the realms of high-level sports, entertainment, teaching, and business. Presence, sensitivity, groundedness, breath, and awareness are the building blocks for mastery in virtually any endeavor. They can be a personal manifesto for your daily life. And many of the pieces and practices I lay out in the following sections will give you exercises that sharpen your own artistry, which you can then bring into your own field of play—day by day, relationship by relationship.

Take Responsibility for Your Own Nourishment

So many men I meet are chronically malnourished. Many are juggling life, community, purpose, and family in some configuration, and the area that most often gets short shrift is the exact place where their souls are most fed. When their Masculine is malnourished, they will naturally start to look for freedom, peace, and relief wherever is most convenient—TV, video games, social media, drugs and alcohol, elaborate vacations, and so on. The impulse is correct, but habits like these don't actually produce the relaxation and rejuvenation most needed. (This is also true for a woman's Masculine.)

In particular, I see a number of men with new children struggle in this way. They want to show up powerfully for their family, yet they are often conflicted by their need to live into their mission and purpose. A positive shift in the past forty years is that more and more men are taking it upon themselves to own a greater stake in parenthood and raising their children. A lot of men have feminine partners who have substantial and successful professional careers as well. It is only right that they take a greater supporting role.

However, this balancing act can be stressful in ways a lot of men don't truly understand. Don't get me wrong—fathers taking a larger role as a nurturing parent is a beautiful by-product of the current landscape, and it is long overdue. However, this dynamic has left men with less time and even more responsibility. Add the distractions of technology, and we have a cocktail of avoidance and numbness masquerading as "downtime."

Four Key Nutrients

The Masculine needs four key nutrients for the nervous system to truly ground and reset. The first is time alone with no demands (which is not the same as meditation). The second is creating time to receive the gifts of the natural world. Third is time spent in depth and reflection with other men (which is even better when there are no demands and nature is involved). I'll address these first three practices now and come back to the fourth shortly, as it involves your feminine partner.

What we are shooting for in this space of no demands is a type of alert relaxation sans numbness. For centuries, men would conclude long periods of hunting or warfare around fires, solely in the company of other men. Quite often, they would do so in nature. They would receive wisdom, tell war stories, tease each other, and let go of any stress or trauma accumulated along the way. This environment of relaxed aliveness encouraged dopamine production and uptake, which then led to heightened levels of testosterone, preparing them for more battles or hunting (and sex, as well).

And these are just the psychophysical needs, not the emotional and soul-soothing aspects of being in the stillness of nature and the company of men who love you but don't want anything from you.

Can we really say the modern man has evolved past these needs? I don't think so. Yet the tried-and-true rituals for this kind of replenishment in relaxed depth have severely waned. I meet men, almost daily, who suffer from some level of depletion brought about by the stress, technology, and responsibility of the modern world. You can see why they are drawn to bars or sporting events together, as these activities at least help provide some of this natural bonding. And while there is absolutely nothing wrong with getting together with your buddies for a couple of beers, most men intuit that it's not the ultimate form of nourishment available to them and that there is a more profound form of masculine connection beyond just hanging out. The common trait I see is a struggle to take full responsibility for owning what will refuel their tanks and inspire them to go back into life's challenges inspired and energized.

Trust me. I know. My favorite excuses are usually some form of "I don't have time," or "my partner gets pissed at me," or "I just can't seem to pull the trigger on taking time for myself." They're all bullshit. Because when pressed to account for how much time is usually spent in frittering away minutes or even hours each day, most men realize it's a matter of prioritization and ownership rather than a time deficit.

So, how exactly do you take full responsibility for your own nourishment? Start by getting clear on your core needs and then commit to filling them like your life depends on it. Because it does. Not only yours, but the health and happiness of those around you. Your capacity to show up with presence and energy will be a direct reflection of how much time you take to get nourished yourself.

PRACTICE IDENTIFY YOUR NEEDS

Take time to reflect on your core needs. Don't judge what comes up or push anything away. Is it time in nature? Exercises that bring you more vitality? Time in silence staring at a wall? Is it more fun and a sense of play? Do you want more time spent in creativity? Is it more connection, intimacy, or passion? Go inside and own what is most important for you. After you identify your needs, choose one or two that feel the most doable right now and schedule ways to address them. If it's time in nature, set aside a morning to hike. If it's more creativity, spend a weekend away focusing on your art or idea. Let those who rely on you know you need a little time to recharge so you can give more of yourself when you come back.

Your feminine partner might not understand your need for nature, other men, and solo time with no demands unless you explain them to her clearly. And then, of course, you show up fully when you return. Try this out some time: "My love, I am depleted and need to get filled so I can be fully present and inspired for our life. I need to get some time alone with God (or nature, or the universe, or the ancestors, or whatever term works for you). How can I support you while I am gone so you feel held? How can we create the same space for you when I get back?"

Now, compare this to suffering silently with your burdens while simultaneously projecting onto her the feeling of being trapped. Conversely, some men rigidly take time without sharing how it will serve the relationship. Or worse, they come home exhausted from partying too hard and are unable to share with their partners the nourishment they received. Both of these dynamics damage her trust in you and can make future discussion of your needs sticky, if not downright contentious.

> If you have unconsciously fallen into a life
> that does not inspire you, it's crucial that you
> find out what you're going to do about it.

Remember, the most important element needed for her to trust and support your quest for freedom and nourishment is knowing that you are seeking depth, stillness, and the divine in some way—not just unconsciously numbing out.

This brings me to the fourth nutrient I mentioned a couple of pages ago. Often the trickiest element of taking responsibility for your own nourishment is making yourself available to the boundless energy in your feminine partner. Chances are—unless there's some significant dysfunction in the relationship—she wants to give you her love, devotion, and sexual energy. She wouldn't be with you otherwise. What she is quite often waiting for is you to create concrete ways for this to happen. This was a revelation for me. "My love, I have to work until 6, but I would love to take a walk on the beach with you after that." (Or make out, cuddle and watch TV, watch her dance, give her a sponge bath, or whatever works for her). "How would that feel to you?" The list is veritably endless if you can both clearly lay out what and when you are available and how her gifts could inspire and nourish you.

The needless tragedy I see is that the feminine desire for connection is often treated as a burden on top of life's grind—not a beautiful opportunity to receive the blessing of feminine devotional and sexual energy. It is possible to feel her need for connection *and* your need for freedom. Doing so will empower you to make your time with her an oasis of energy, mutual worship, and devotion rather than a neutered landscape of tasks and duties. This will energize you, inspire her, and open a much more nourishing set of possibilities in your relationship.

Create a Life That Inspires You First

If you have unconsciously fallen into a life that does not inspire you, it's crucial that you find out what you're going to do about it. It's far too easy to place the blame on others (your spouse and children, for example, or your lack thereof), your job, your debt, and so on. Maybe you've lost sight of the life you wanted for yourself because you spent too much time chasing money, love, duty, or some other unconscious impulse. Did you become a doctor because your father was one? Or reject his path and become an entrepreneur because he was a corporate lifer? Did you pick up addictions along the way that have limited your life? Have you been chasing feminine attention rather than addressing what truly frees your soul? So many of our life choices get made unconsciously, as we live out the momentum of our (and our parents') histories and expectations.

The pressures to domesticate and start consuming are constant and real, and they're centuries old. If we don't stop and look ourselves squarely in the eye and ask, "What are my *Hell Yeses* and *Hell Noes*?" (more on those below), then those pressures will often take hold, and we will find ourselves trying on roles to please others, not ourselves. It's a prison, albeit sometimes a golden one. But it will not inspire us or benefit those around us in the long run.

My ex-wife would always want me to go to gatherings of her family and friends, which, being the dutiful husband, I usually did. They were often on weekends, and I had just started a new business and worked six days a week. On top of that, my daughter had special needs and spent a lot of time in the hospital. By Sunday, all I wanted to do was take some time to rest and restore before reentering the week ahead—surf, hike, sleep, watch movies, or hang out with my buddies. But I rarely did any of this. Instead, I put on a role that didn't fit and ignored what I needed to feel inspired in my life. My partner was just doing what Feminine love-driven beings do: create space for connection and love. Unfortunately, I grew resentful and blamed her for my lack of freedom and my habit of avoiding what made me happy to be alive. Even worse, I punished her with silent resentment and neglect—all because I didn't have the conscious awareness and skill set to take full responsibility for what kind of Sunday I needed in order to feel alive and ready to show up for not only her, but the world. And, of course, there is nothing wrong with your spouse's family gatherings. Especially if you're taking care of yourself otherwise and those gatherings also feed you in some way.

The Feminine requires a man to be in true alignment with his heart if she is going to trust him with all of hers. This statement will confuse a lot of men. It certainly confused me. "But it's important to her that I show up at her family gatherings," I thought. It's actually more important to your partner that you be in complete integrity with your heart. That you honor your own needs for nourishment, freedom, play, and connection to the Infinite. From this place of fullness and alignment, you can choose where and how to support her and do it wholeheartedly, with maximum presence and commitment. All of this needs to be balanced. Her needs for nourishment, your needs for freedom from demands, and the flow of love that makes the relationship a place of healing for you both.

Another way that I see men lose alignment in this area is to mistakenly attempt to find the right partner, the right job, or the right life situation before truly clarifying and landing in the space of inspired living and purpose. Unfortunately, it works the other way around. If you attract these people and things in your life from a place of confusion and internal conflict, don't be alarmed by who and what shows up. Most men choose the comfort of relationship or job security over the fire of learning what they are on the planet to do, only to have to unwind and recalibrate later while committed to the responsibilities of a relationship.

It's far better to hunt the purpose, depth, and lifestyle you crave with the strongest, most direct intention *and then* invite her into your world as an invaluable partner and ally. From this place, you are your most attractive and magnetic. Trust me. She can relax and feel completely aligned with you because you are in a space of knowing what you are here to do. I am, of course, not implying you need to have it all figured out before entering a job or relationship, but the priority needs to be on your core truth, as opposed to sexual and material comfort. Those will come in time if you are aligned and living in true integrity with yourself.

PRACTICE **OWN YOUR *HELL YESES* AND *HELL NOES***

There's a beautiful practice I learned from my friend Rich Litvin that's called "Hell Yes, Hell No, and Maybe." If you aren't clear about what's inspiring you versus draining you, this exercise will help immediately.

First, write down in capital letters at the top of a clean sheet of paper, HELL YES. Then start listing all the activities and projects and passions that fit in this category. You will immediately start to feel good just turning your attention to addressing this topic. Be generous with yourself. Is it someone you'd like to date? A project you want to start? A friendship you want more of? A teacher you want to study with? An adventure you want to have? Listing your Hell Yeses is a crucial act of honoring yourself, and it needs consciousness and total commitment. Surfing with buddies, hiking in nature, writing this book, working with certain teachers, and mornings with hours free to practice and meditate are all examples of mine. Once you have identified your Hell Yeses, bring this list to your trusted friends and commit to creating more space and attention for these activities. Let them know how important your Hell Yeses are for you, and ask them to hold you to making them more central to your life.

Next, on the top of a second clean piece of paper, write in capital letters, HELL NO. Underneath that header write the activities, responsibilities, habits, toxic relationships, and situations that are clear noes for you. These might include work responsibilities you'd just rather not be doing, ways you have of fighting with your partner, or addictions you know have to go. Be ruthlessly self-reflective and honest. Then share your HELL NO list with some friends you trust and begin to make a clear and steadfast commitment to get the hell out of them as soon as possible. This list will tell you exactly what's sucking the life force from you. And the only person who can change it is you. Once you clear the space of the things that don't align with your own truth, there is space for a whole new set of possibilities that turn you on.

Finally, on a third sheet of paper, write in capital letters MAYBE. Then, list all of the activities, habits, responsibilities, and relationships that are just okay—in other words, they neither inspire nor repulse you. They are just kind of *blah* things in your life that you tolerate because something is telling you that you should. Perhaps you feel obligated or duty bound, or you're afraid you'll lose someone's love if you don't comply. *Maybe* is the area where most of us waste far too much time. We commit to things that are not quite what we really need or crave—often because there is some comfort payoff or fear of change. Leave yourself some space in between each Maybe on the list, because I want you to ask another question: "What would have to happen for this to become a solid HELL YES?" Then clearly write out your answer. (For example, "I would need to work thirty hours per week on this project so I could have time to pursue _____ ," or "I would need my girlfriend to bring more _____ ," or "I would need more integrity and tough love from my men's group to be inspired to continue _____ .")

There are almost always clear needs that will move a MAYBE to a HELL YES. And if you can't find them, move it to the HELL NO category and find a way to cut it loose. This is your life, brother. Get clear and own it.

Know Your Nonnegotiable Needs in Relationship

A similar but more nuanced concept is owning what's negotiable for you in a relationship as well as what's not. Even better is knowing what the core needs are beneath your nonnegotiables. For example, you might have an undeniable need for sexual depth in your romantic life that goes beyond a simple desire for more sex. I see in many men (and women) the need for a richer, more conscious, fully expressed sexuality. You might have a need for uncompromising devotion, adventure, and travel, or for your partner to trust you fully. Whatever your need, on the other side is a nonnegotiable term in your relationship.

Think about it. If you need sexual and emotional devotion, polyamory is likely not for you. If you need fully expressed sexuality in your marriage, your sexual practice and exploration will go beyond simple desire. Your needs are important nutrients for your heart and soul, and you will invariably feel weaker when they aren't met. They aren't things you can sleep on or leave to chance if you want to be happy and fully expressed, because needs must be acknowledged, nurtured, prioritized, and scheduled. You will have to bring consciousness and intention to them, and then co-create with your partner to clarify what your nonnegotiables are.

Here is where I will often see men go blank, as most of us have not been taught to own our core truths and get crystal clear on what we need. Not to mention how to take 100 percent responsibility for manifesting it in our lives. And so we fall into a victim story. "My wife doesn't appreciate all that I do," or "I wish she would wear a sexy outfit for me the way she used to," or "My boyfriend doesn't trust my decision-making or leadership anymore." We *complain* rather than feeling the purity of our beautiful human needs at the base of these complaints: The need for sexual energy as a gift. The need for the feminine being you love to trust your direction. The need for devotion. The need for physical affection. The need for space from demands. These needs are not problems; they're not arguable. Not clarifying these needs too often results in bitterness and emotional withdrawal, which is a tragedy that leaches the love force from even the most powerful connection.

The way this showed up in my life is that during a particularly difficult period of stress with my partner of many years ago, our fights started to devolve into name calling and insults. It was horrible. Neither of us meant it, but we both had tempers and felt justified in our positions. Maybe this sounds familiar. The fights with my ex continued to worsen, and our relationship was on the brink. One day, as I was complaining about it in my men's group (something like "how dare she continue to disrespect me this way!"), a friend of mine said, "It sounds like you have a nonnegotiable term in your relationship that you will not disrespect or insult each other. Ever. Especially when trying to work out disagreements. Is that correct?"

As soon as he said it, I felt the simple and powerful truth of it. That wasn't who I wanted to be. Nor her, for that matter. I wasn't serving our love by letting our fights devolve into that shit show, and I quickly realized that I had compromised a key term—a crucial nonnegotiable need for me in any love relationship: honor and respect. It wasn't her fault, as she had her own childhood wounds she was trying to heal. It was my own lack of awareness to what was truly important to me and what

I was prepared to fight for. I had compromised myself and her, and I apologized for both letting myself and her behave so dishonorably. I also committed to her that from then on, any name-calling or insults would not be tolerated by either of us.

But I had to go further. I couldn't stop at just saying I was sorry. I knew the momentum of our childhood wounds, our family karmas, and the dynamic we had already developed would need much more structure and discipline if things were to really change. So, I set a boundary. I requested that from then on, if we had any resentments, disagreements, or hurt feelings, we must have an intentional dialogue (a tried-and-true Imago Therapy practice that prioritizes empathy, validation, and reflective listening). I proposed that no matter what, when either of us started to become upset, we would call for a dialogue and the other party would have to respect it. It was the only way to break that horrid dynamic, and we were better than that. Then I apologized again for not being clear enough earlier and for not putting a stop to the pain we were causing one another.

Her heart immediately relaxed and melted open. She cried and thanked me for being so willing to stand for our love. It was a moment of victory for me, as I had no idea this kind of radical responsibility and heart-centered polarity would evoke the kind of love we shared. Until our next fight, that is. When she responded to my call for a dialogue in a way that any wild-hearted, powerful, sovereign feminine being might when a man steps in to tell her that things are becoming too heated and that everybody should take a step back, tone it down, and engage in compassionate dialogue. She said, "Fuck you, asshole! Don't try to control me!" (Or something to that effect.)

> Boundary setting is an art and discipline that
> takes clarity, fortitude, and compassion.

Holding the line in that moment was one of the hardest decisions I have ever made. I was crazy in love with her, but I couldn't allow that dynamic to continue. I was clear that I was not willing to compromise a core need in me, no matter how heated a disagreement got. We were not to name-call or character-assassinate each other. We had to stop, take a breath, and commit to a practice of empathy, understanding, and love. Or let each other go (which is what we did).

Set Boundaries in Service of Love

A boundary provides structure, protection, and direction to emotions or behaviors. At its core, it's a conscious container for energy. Whoever sets a boundary is holding the masculine pole at that moment. For this reason, an important part of masculine leadership is to not only set boundaries but provide a clear plan that supports seeing them through. So, if you want your feminine partner to relax into your boundary and trust you wholeheartedly, there needs to be direction, clarity, and structure to the request (as opposed to a simple demand).

Because boundaries honor needs that inevitably serve and nourish the relationship, the fact that someone calls for one is a sign that they want to remain in the relationship and that they need a bottom line met in order to do so. Conversely, if one partner compromises a true core need, then the relationship is fatally flawed and will eventually collapse. So, setting a boundary is an act of commitment, regardless of which partner proposes it. The problems that come from setting boundaries are typically about how they are expressed or upheld, as opposed to the needs they're meant to address.

Boundary setting is an art and discipline that takes clarity, fortitude, and compassion. Using boundaries to shift a relational dynamic—especially one that's habitually well grooved—takes an unwavering intention that may require months or years of effort.

I eventually reconciled with the partner discussed at the end of the last segment. She agreed to create a plan with me that would help us communicate our feelings and love each other more artfully. We found an Imago therapist, practiced daily dialogues for months, and eventually became so good at them that we taught the practice to others. I have now taught this practice to hundreds of couples who found themselves in similar situations to me. None of this would have happened if I hadn't been determined to honor what I knew was true for both me and her.

Taking full responsibility for what I needed and holding to those needs as clearly and artfully as I could had ripple effects I could have never imagined. This is the often-unrecognized power of honoring core needs and then creating a real plan to execute them—an act of self-love that has the power to elevate any relationship to its highest potential (or expedite its completion). Either way, the personal integrity you stand to gain is a priceless gift.

Feel Your Partner's Deepest Needs and Desires

Simply put, the primary masculine gift in any relationship is conscious, embodied awareness. Once you can clearly identify and feel your own core needs, you can turn your awareness toward others from a place of love and integrity. With this intention, you can simultaneously own your core need to be trusted (for example) *and* her profound need to feel safe. This is the yogic practice of feeling both of your hearts in any moment and allowing something fresh to emerge that creates a whole new possibility of connection and depth.

We will get more into the nuances of what this looks like in a bit. For now, suffice to say the proper use of your awareness is to feel, witness, amplify, and liberate more love between you. That is what healthy masculine leadership means in the context of relational work. It's about liberation of her love, not simply personal satisfaction. This is a primary masculine responsibility in any relationship with the Feminine—be it romantic, parental, or communal.

The intentional decision to step into this role means that you are making the commitment to pay meticulous attention to her needs, desires, and yearnings. Maybe even more than she does at times. This also means you will become an unwavering advocate for her without abandoning your own core truths and needs. That is love. That is service and devotion. What I am describing here is the difference between simply falling in love and committing to lead a feminine being in love—assuming, of course, that she wants that. Some don't, although many do, and part of succeeding in relationships as a man is being able to understand the difference.

Remember, tuning in to another's needs is a skill—like so many of the other relational practices I offer in this book. It is a meditation of feeling and awareness that requires you to expand beyond self and feel into another body and heart. Like any artform, it takes intention, commitment, and practice. Not to mention a willingness to fail and course correct.

For example, suppose your wife comes home from work and immediately shifts into mother and domestic partner mode by cleaning up or directing the kids. Perhaps you can sense that she is dropping into her habitual roles and responsibilities, but because you are tuned in to her, you can also feel that her heart is weary, her body is tense, her breath is shallow, and her movements are fast and sharp. This is the perfect opportunity to intuit what she truly needs, be it a bath and some time to herself, your hand on her heart for five minutes, a tender kiss, or a kind ear as she releases some of her sadness or frustration from the day. Your attentive presence and ability to guide her into the space of true feeling will occur to her nervous system as love. All you have to do is to pay attention to her breath and body, and then trust your instinct.

This capacity becomes invaluable during sex. Perhaps she needs tender and slow lovemaking, or maybe it's quite the opposite. Maybe she longs to be ravished from a darker side of you, consumed with such raw passion that she surrenders her conceptualizing and just gives in utterly to the moment. It doesn't take a genius to know that being able to discern these needs will increase your esteem as a valuable and healing lover. Assuming that you're willing, of course.

The masculine gift in relationship is liberation.

There have certainly been times in my life when I could only attend to myself, and if you can't be responsible for another's body and heart (or don't want to), the least you can do is acknowledge the fact and communicate it clearly. This is a crucial piece of masculine integrity in relationship. To own fully whether you want to love her this deeply or are just in the habit of being together. One will inspire her (and you) into a more sublime devotion to each other's growth and healing, and one will result in staleness or even resentment. What I am asking is that you find the place in you that wants to feel her needs and desires every day, or let her go so she can find someone who wants to offer her that gift.

Take a Stand for Her, Even If She Hates You Momentarily

The feminine paradox that dumbfounds many men (it certainly did me) is that your feminine partner will both crave your heartfelt, conscious leadership and likewise resist it. This is true for your Feminine as well. Think about it. The raging river is guided artfully by huge rocks but is also always trying to overwhelm them. Your work will be to understand if this resistance comes from wisdom and self-care or fear and habitual self-protection. She could, of course, do the same for you. If it's the latter, then you must have the fortitude to unrelentingly help her through any contractions in her heart and back to love. That's the fundamental value you offer as a masculine partner.

If you truly love a highly feminine being and have begun to cultivate the sensitivity and awareness to feel her intensely, then there will be times when you know her heart is closed—maybe just to you, or quite possibly to the world. This may feel like tension in her body, neurotic thought looping, rage, or some other form of negativity that she can't seem to shake. Maybe some of her pain is connected to past wounds and you can sense that, as well. Just as she can likely see when you are shut down, you'll also know when something needs to shift for her to remember that she, as a primarily feminine being, is (at her core) love itself.

Remember, the masculine gift in relationship is liberation. From excessive thought, from stress, from closure. And your capacity to assist her into a space of openness and love is priceless. Perhaps she just needs to dance for a half hour, scream and pound a pillow, take a nap, make love feverishly, jump in the ocean, or spend a weekend with her friends. If you have been tuning into her body and heart, you'll know. And, over time, you'll develop even more capacity to intuit what she needs to return to the essence of love she is.

That said, don't expect her to immediately (or happily) take to your suggestion. If she did not receive a trustable masculine imprint when she was young, she will likely struggle to trust any masculine figure in her life (even her own). She may fiercely resist your attempts to help her through the pain or confusion of the moment.

Knowing what she needs is one thing. Having the presence, depth, artful perseverance, and stamina to take her where she needs to be is often quite another. If she is in some karmic, habitual quagmire, then you are combatting years, if not generations, of well-established grooves in her nervous system. Even so, true leadership in service of love requires not buying into her pattern—just as you hope she won't allow you to buy into your own patterns of burden, overthinking, numbness, and closure.

To be committed as a masculine partner means that you are an immovable stand for her open heart and body, even when she's actively testing your resolve. Her and your patterns have tentacles that extend into your hearts and spines in ways we still don't totally understand. Ego structures—both hers and yours—unwind and break down stubbornly, so when the inevitable resistance to your heartfelt direction arises, what will you do? This is where most men collapse, check out, or get lazy. They will adhere to the unhelpful belief that she is quite capable of leading herself out of the rut, and they'll leave her to sort the issue out by herself. Here's where many men just remove themselves from the situation, and with predictable results.

Chances are that she absolutely can lead herself back to openness, although it may not be nearly as pleasurable for her. And the moment she steps in to handle herself, she has to summon up the resources of her own Masculinity, which also means that the sexual polarity you have worked so hard to establish in your relationship will be neutralized.

What if you took 100 percent responsibility for her openness, freedom, and joy? Imagine your partner has been clinging to a particular resentment even after you have apologized and talked it out multiple times. You can intuit that she needs to move this through her body and fully express the level of pain she has been carrying. "My love, take three minutes and show me with your body and sound only how angry and hurt you are. No more talking about it. I will just be the conscious witness to you and not say anything." Your feminine partner may resist you, because she's still hurting and doesn't trust you fully. But try holding firm. Tell her, "We aren't going anywhere until you reveal all of your hurt to me. I want to hold space for what you are carrying, even if its resentment toward me." The healing power of your willingness and ability to love these parts of her will be a revelation for both of you.

This is the moment of truth. Do you love her enough to hold the pose and not accept anything other than the full embodied revealing of her heart? Or will you cave to her resistance and build your own resentment against her? She may yell at you and tell you to back off. Just smile, tell her you love her, and offer to wait all night if it will help her move through her pain. Eventually, feeling the depth of your judgment-free love, and your unwavering stand for her full expression, trust will emerge and she will let it fly. Maybe she'll scream, stomp, move her body around, and even pound on your chest. But your deep breath, soft eyes, and grounded presence will comfort her. Your intention is unbendable. Eventually, her anger will turn to anguish and she may cry or collapse in your arms. This is not an uncommon scene.

The problem is that most men cannot metabolize the emotions surrounding their partner's mistrust to being firmly, but lovingly, led into openness. They will either run from her anger, meet it with their own, or use the excuse that she is "her own woman" all in order to avoid the presence and meticulous care that's being called for.

How committed to your partner's open heart and body are you? Are you willing to withstand her momentary anger at your nonnegotiable gesture of love, or will you let her convince you in a habitual moment of closure that presence and love are not needed? I guarantee you, if her essence is truly Feminine, she's hoping you will hold firm to your conviction above her closure. She is hoping, day after day, that you will help unburden her heart when she gets overwhelmed by life's inevitable pain. She is hoping you will lead her out of the habits of closure that hide her full radiance. That is why she chose you.

Assume Full Responsibility for the Culture You Have Created

It takes tremendous courage, depth, insight, and ruthless honesty to look at where you have been neglectful, unconscious, selfish, stingy, and maybe even abusive in some way. And great leadership in any endeavor entails a willingness to take full responsibility for the state of any situation.

Many people do not have the constitution to truly look at how they have created or have allowed an unhealthy culture to take hold in their love dynamics. For many, it requires ruthlessly reflecting on their own choices and compromises. As a result, some will either push too hard and try to impose their will on their partners with blame and shame, or will quietly ignore the most important issues of the relationship and turn their attention in a direction where they are more apt to win. But dysfunction has a way of revealing itself over time.

Unhealthy ecosystems often take time to develop, even decades. For example, you may have allowed you and your partner to co-create a relational culture of complaint, as opposed to a culture of honor and worship. Rather than agreements and structures that support each other with heartfelt and sincere requests, you complain at one another about the needs that aren't getting met. Maybe you've turned a blind eye to this process and then wonder why you and your lover aren't sexually attracted to each other. Maybe your fights turn abusive—verbally, emotionally, and—even worse—physically. Maybe your complaints become cruel character assassinations. Maybe you blame each other for everything negative that's developed.

There are also relational cultures of avoidance, spiritual bypassing, emotional dishonesty, and so on. What's important here is to bring sharp awareness and honesty to what you have allowed to take root in your space. See it clearly and name it. Is it the most loving version of your relationship? Is it the most artful expression of who you both are? The most generous and understanding? The most adventurous and exploratory? You are free to choose what you value most and prioritize it. The problem is that many men unconsciously allow things that aren't aligned with their highest values to dictate the tone and direction of their relationships, and then they wonder why they are dissatisfied, numb, or feel trapped.

> Change will only happen when you model how to take a completely different stance in the dynamic.

A couple I worked with was at an all-time low after ten years of marriage with three children. He made money, took care of himself physically, was a dedicated father, and was loved in his community—a living example of the "Myth of the Good Husband." On the surface, the two were a picture of the all-American couple. Yet he had allowed the passion and intimacy in his relationship to wither to such a degree that they were barely having sex. A powerful and successful woman in her own right, his wife became increasingly depressed and angry at his lack of care and attention. As a result, they fought bitterly.

The first thing I did was to encourage him to take complete responsibility for the state and culture of the relationship. I said, "Stop looking at her and take 100 percent responsibility for the culture *you* have allowed to take hold. If she is complaining, feel into why. If you are not interested in sex, get clear on what you are missing. Survey the entire field and make a plan." The moment he stepped up and said, "I have allowed this to go on for too long, you are the mother of our children and my wife, and I love you," their whole dynamic changed. He led intimate communication practices that helped them clear years of resentments, and he created space for them to enjoy sex. He reset the entire relationship in a matter of weeks, and she was moved to tears of gratitude.

Whatever the dysfunction, *you*, the masculine partner, must take full responsibility. You model what it looks like to be in pristine integrity and meticulous reflection. Your partner will likely be inspired and follow your lead. This is just as true if the woman is the predominant masculine partner in a relationship. Not because the other partner doesn't play a role, but because change will only happen when you model how to take a completely different stance in the dynamic. It's a tough exercise, but it's also the surest way to completely reset a relationship and develop a fresh new culture of love, respect, mutual worship, and sexual intimacy. Feel the difference between, "This isn't working, all we do is fight and complain," and "I am sorry, my love, I have allowed us to get into the habit of complaining and blaming each other for way too long. Here are the ways in which I have let us down (then, of course, list what you have discovered after heartfelt, ruthless reflection, ideally involving men you trust). This has to stop. And here is my plan for us." Totally different, yes?

PRACTICE **THREE-STEP DIALOGUE**

Here is the basic structure I have developed to help reset and guide a relationship out of a toxic culture and into a dynamic of healing and love. You can, of course, amend this to fit your situation. But, as a tested framework, the following three steps work quite well.

Appraise.

Whoever is the predominant Masculine energy in the relationship must take a ruthless and fearless appraisal as to how *they* have allowed the relationship to devolve into an unhealthy and possibly abusive relationship. If you are reading this book, chances are that is you.

Have you let your sexual connection wither? Have you allowed the way you speak to each other be filled with contempt rather than respect? Have you created structures that nourish the relationship, or have you been lazy? Have you been selfish? Have you allowed them to be selfish and remained silent so as to not rock the boat? Do you really listen to each other and honor the other's experiences and feedback? Or do you make each other's feelings, beliefs, and emotional experiences a problem? Have you taken for granted or rejected each other's innate masculine and feminine gifts? Do you criticize each other or hold grudges? Or, worse, have you let violence or abuse creep in? Do you each have space and time to get nourished—separately and together? Think about these questions through the lens of what you have not made a true stance to own and change.

This is best done with other men who will shine a different light on your dynamic and hold you accountable for the areas in which you have been unconsciously allowing your relationship to drift.

Share and Own.

Have a conversation, or series of conversations, in which you own what you have let take hold in the relationship. Leading from this place means you will keep the focus on your behavior. Highlight your selfishness, laziness, numbness, and lack of consciousness, illuminating the ways you have allowed love to devolve into contempt, apathy, neglect, or abuse. You must make this about you taking full responsibility, even if your partner's behavior hasn't been stellar. You allowed the conditions for that behavior to fester due to your inaction, fear, or lethargy, and it is best to approach it from that angle. For example, "I didn't call you out when you said unkind things about me in front of the children. I should have made a stand long ago, and that is on me." Feel the difference from that statement and, "You belittle and degrade me in front of the children."

This is a conversation that models what it means to take complete responsibility from pristine awareness. It is about you bringing a clarifying consciousness to what has really happened to cause disconnection and unhappiness. You might not be completely spot on, and you will likely still play out some of the unprocessed wounds of your childhood, but your sincere efforts will inspire trust, empathy, and quite often her own self-reflection.

You will need to be clear on where you may have sacrificed your most sacred values or terms in the relationship. Is a core value of yours to have a passionate and connected sex life? That you never criticize or curse each other? Are completely honest about resentments and desires? That you have adventure and travel as part of your life?

If you allow your deepest values to be compromised or neglected, whose fault is that? Take clear responsibility for not only allowing these values to become disavowed but also your tendency to blame your partner for it. I see this in many men who suffer from what Robert Glover calls "the Nice Guy Syndrome." Nobody wins by you withholding your truths and allowing your most sacred values to be compromised.

Finally, make sure to fill this conversation with empathy. What has it been like for her? Feel the impact of your behaviors, habits, and numbness. How has your partner's health, happiness, and emotional well-being suffered as a result of your unconsciousness? Have the guts to look at this and own how your behavior—conscious or not—has caused pain or even despair and hopelessness.

A typical example I have seen is the unconscious use of porn. Rather than create a nourishing sex life with their partners, some men rely on the fantasy, numbness, distraction, and expediency readily available online. Rather than become truly committed practitioners of sexual intimacy, they have opted for quick stress release.

A man taking this inventory and approach will be able to feel into what it must be like for a love-driven being. How has this pain penetrated your partner's heart? How might she be turning your habit into a belief about herself? Does she feel unattractive, hopeless, or abandoned? If you brought your open heart and pristine awareness to the full impact of this behavior, it would break your heart. Do it anyway. And then let her feel your new broken-hearted fierceness and determination to give more.

Scan your relationship for any places you know you have brought less than your greatest intention for love. Feel into where she has been exhausted, felt dropped, unseen, and unsupported. This is not about blaming or shaming yourself. It is a warrior's reflection of personal integrity, and it will evoke a trust in devotion in her you may never have experienced.

For her to completely trust you, a blanket apology won't do. You must make a stand for love from the most powerful space of your heart. It is also a magnificent opportunity for you to show her that you truly understand and feel what her feminine experience must have been like all of these months or years. This is a legitimately healing experience for a love-driven being. To be seen and known fully is at the core of the Feminine heart's desires.

Finally, let her know you have thought about a path forward (or will have one shortly) and will of course want to make sure it feels good to her. Let her know it is your priority to change this dynamic so that love, respect, worship, and generosity (or whatever values are most called for) become the predominant traits of your experience together. You can share the broad strokes in this conversation, but it is often best to have another conversation using the structure I lay out in the next step.

Transform and Repair.

This is where you create a plan to transform your relationship culture with her. Now that you have reestablished a deeper trust and shown incredible capacity as a man who can be completely trusted, you have an opportunity to craft a new direction for you both. Please don't take this lightly. This is the point where you can step up and change the relationship karmas (the destinies) of all involved, including your children.

What will you have to prioritize so that you can have a different experience together? Will you commit to couples therapy or take a workshop together to enhance your sexual intimacy? Should one of you address an underlying issue— perhaps anger or trauma—separately in therapy? Do you need to sell your business and travel the world? Do you need to hire a nanny? Do you need to lose weight together? Do you each need more space apart? Separate rooms for your personal practices? Whatever the direction, come up with a well-considered plan. Then, say something like, "Here is what I want for us, my love. . . . How does it feel to you?"

Then listen. Watch her body. Does it relax or tense? Does she take a deep breath or hold her breath? She might like part of the plan, but not another. Take all of her feedback of your leadership not as a criticism but as an expression of her heart's yearning to trust and love you. And then adjust and update your plan accordingly.

This may take a few rounds of offering your vision and then getting her feedback. But at the conclusion you will have co-created a beautiful path forward with you taking the lead. This is one of the most important things a feminine being wants—to be led deeper into the experience of love by a masculine partner, a man of ruthless integrity and self-reflection.

There will, of course, be unconscious resistance from both of you. There will be life shit that stalls or waylays your plans. Stay the course and adjust as obstacles arise. You are like a sailor traveling from Los Angeles to New Zealand—storms may come and knock you off course, but you sensitively adjust to the weather while enjoying the beauty of the journey. After all, getting to New Zealand is great, but the journey is what you'll remember forever.

This practice, fully engaged, has immense power to change the destiny and direction of any relationship. I have seen it work with families, companies, and lovers. Any relationship that has been unhealthy or toxic can be healed if the Masculine is willing to reflect, change, and lead in this way.

Mastering Meticulous Communication

Once you have become more sensitive to your own core truth, the truth of her heart, the flow of love between you, and the strength of your foundation together, you must learn how to meticulously and clearly communicate what you see and feel will best serve not only the relationship and each other, but the world you live in. You must create structures she can trust that will allow her to fully reveal what she feels is true and important. It's one thing to say, "Why are you mad now?" and quite another to say, "I am sensing some tension building between us; let's have a dialogue." Noticing the wobble caused by uncleared tension or resentment in the field is important. But having a way to clear it out so that both of you feel met and seen is a powerful part of the Masculine's leadership.

Like so much in this work, meticulous communication is a practice, an art, a skill to master. I use the word *meticulous* throughout this book because it is one of the primary tenets of conscious masculinity. As the samurai adorns his robe to perfection, or a shaman constructs a sacred space with painstaking care, the conscious Masculine generates containers that allow energy to flow and love to blossom. Carlos Castaneda once said that creating spaces of power requires everything to be perfect. This is as true for a sacred ritual like marriage, an important conversation, or a night of deep lovemaking. Unconscious sloppiness is the enemy of depth. So, if you want your clearings to be open, honest, and powerful, then your structures must be as pristine as possible. Then she can completely relax into trusting you.

There are numerous communication techniques available—the Intentional Dialogue of Imago Therapy I mentioned in my personal story earlier, for example, or Marshall Rosenberg's Nonviolent Communication (NVC). Each style has its own way of encouraging the flow of truth between partners and other important relationships. Each has a clear and solid structure that if followed will encourage the flow of empathy and love between you. I recommend trying at least two or three of them, because the more arrows you have in your quiver, the more effortless and artful your exchanges will become.

It is the Masculine's responsibility to find ways to meet both your needs and hers, and the way in which you communicate each of your needs means everything. Feel the difference between, "You aren't giving me_____" and "I am finding I need _____ in our relationship, and this is how I would love you to give it to me." Your awareness, consciousness, and clarity in the words you employ and how you deliver them will determine the quality of openness between you. The difference between speaking off-the-cuff on important matters and communicating meticulously could be the difference between unconsciously expecting your lover to mother you and consciously co-creating your relationship with them.

One practice I often use is a simple revealing practice with reflection and empathy. Withholding, judging, and resenting build mistrust and create distance between people, and they are mostly unnecessary to begin with. When your feminine partner knows they can bring anything to you, and that you will hold and honor what they have to share, they will invariably relax into a space of deep trust, which is the cornerstone of any devotional relationship. So, when you experience anything that could harm trust and connection, try the following practice, which is adopted from the Imago Dialogue.

PRACTICE REVEALING RESENTMENTS

One partner begins by revealing their resentment or judgment. For example, they may tell you, "When you say you will be home at 6 p.m. and you come home at 8 p.m., I feel resentful and mistrustful of you. I judge you as someone who is flaky and won't keep your word." In this example, you would reflect their words back to them using as much of their language as possible. Then check in with them to make sure you got it, and ask if there's anything more they'd like to add. If so, repeat these steps until they have expressed themselves fully. After they've done that, it's time to express how you think it might feel to be in their shoes. "I imagine you feel disappointed when I keep you waiting or don't show up when I say I will. I imagine you feel resentful that I am not home to help with the kids and you have to hold the fort down without me. I imagine you wonder if you can truly trust me." Spend a few minutes sincerely reflecting how it must feel for them and then ask, "Did I miss anything?" As always, listen carefully and clearly to what they say.

Basically, that's it. You can use this same practice to share desires, praise, feelings you've withheld, and so on. The space you share can be for the sake of resentments and judgments, or you can infuse it with appreciation, praise, and love.

These are the healthy masculine communication containers that will build trust and respect between you. Although some of what they share may have some sting to it, the fact that you have offered a structured container to hold it will make them feel incredibly grateful and more trusting of you. And your Feminine—which also needs to be seen and heard fully—will relax even more knowing you will also be heard and loved in whatever you bring. This is a crucial part of the culture you are creating with your partner, in which needs and truths are honored and expressed with love and acceptance.

Embrace Feminine Criticism (from Her and the World) as a Way to Gauge How Conscious You Are

One of the most underappreciated gifts a feminine being can offer is their innate ability to reflect when and where you go unconscious. And when this takes the form of subtle (or not so subtle) criticisms and complaints, it can prove painful and confusing, especially if you don't understand the source of their pain.

> She truly yearns for you to live as the embodiment
> of masculine awareness and integrity.

The common masculine response to any complaint or criticism is to defend, deflect, or react in similar fashion. That's normal. I spent years defending myself against my partner's complaints whenever I thought she was being harsh or overly critical, only to discover years later that her comments were actually pointing out my numbness and lack of awareness. She regularly showed me how I was getting caught up in my head (usually to think about myself) and how I would often check out or fall short in keeping my word. Granted, she wasn't always particularly artful in how she shared her feelings with me, but once I understood what was at the root of her unhappiness, it became clear that her desire was simply more consciousness, more sensitivity, and more love. Of course, she wanted that. Why wouldn't she?

The reframe that will change everything for you is the assumption that her complaints and criticisms are coming from the same place: that she truly yearns for you to live as the embodiment of masculine awareness and integrity. I assure you that assuming she's nagging for no good reason will only lead to bitterness and disconnection. The sensitivity of her demanding heart is your ally, not a villain. She is much more capable of knowing when you are off course than you are most of the time, as it will show up in her body as pain, confusion, anxiety, and subtle heartache. So, when you leave the toilet seat up or fail to deliver on a promise, her body will feel it. She may often not know why, but she might direct the sensations at you in sometimes unfavorable ways because she can sense that you, in one way or another, are a condition or cause of her suffering. And maybe you are.

What's the big deal about the toilet seat, anyway? A valid question, but only if she were actually complaining about your behavior in the bathroom. Which, of course, she isn't. What she's pointing out is how inconsiderate you can be at times or how you've failed to fulfill an agreed-upon responsibility. You have lost awareness of her and others because of your laziness to just put down the damn seat. No judgment here. Guilty of it many times. Until I realized she just wanted me to be more conscientious and aware. So, if you forget such things, it could very well signify to her that she can't trust you to show up as promised. If you can't keep your word, how can she trust you to be a good husband and father?

These concerns and assessments can come across as unfair or crazy to most masculine-identified people. Her nervous system can't relax until she can feel the expanse of your awareness and presence again.

Remember that at her core she wants to trust you completely with her heart and life, and that she wouldn't be with you otherwise. So, when you forget to put the toilet seat down, it's not just some surface issue for her. It actually encourages her to doubt your capacity to love and protect her.

Consider a different approach: The next time your partner (or whatever you call the Feminine in your life) complains—even if it occurs as trivial to you—ask yourself the following questions: Where is she right? Did I drop something habitually that didn't take her or those around me into consideration? Was I lazy or checked out? Do I have a history of doing this? What is at the core of her upset, assuming that it goes beyond a surface-level complaint?

Feel into the less apparent layers of her heart and ruthlessly reflect on where she may be pointing to something that would make you a more trustable, more integral person. Not just in your relationship but in the world. What if her feedback is the whetstone that sharpens your blade? The training that widens your awareness and the call for you to be the best you can be in this lifetime? Would that change your relationship to her feedback? Could you even begin to feel profound gratitude? Could you become more playful and curious? Consider that she is in your life to call out more of the best in you, not just to cut you down.

Once you feel the truth of this, it's way easier to respond and make amends, because the critique doesn't carry the same charge. When you acknowledge how you have dropped your awareness and then show her you can remain open and relaxed, it will change everything. A simple "My bad, love—that was unconscious of me" will go a long way. Moments like these add up to create more energy and sexual polarity between you, and they become the foundation of trust your relationship can be built upon rather than a misperceived attack on your character.

Know Where You're Withholding Your Gifts

It's crucial that you determine where you aren't being present, clear, integral, and loving in your work, relationship, life at home, and so on. Think about what gifts you could bring to your partner and the world that would promote healing, opening, and relaxation if you held nothing back. You may find that you are stingy at home with your full presence or that you ignore certain people in your business rather than give them direction on how to succeed. Or perhaps you are selfish during sex and habitually steer lovemaking in the direction of your climax. Maybe financially you withhold your resources. Are you cheap? Do you weaponize money against your spouse and children? Perhaps you withhold your own vulnerabilities for fear you will be judged or abandoned.

> True personal responsibility requires us to constantly reflect on where we are withholding and falling short.

This exploration requires a ruthless assessment of how you are showing up in the world and for what reasons, and to this end I strongly recommend enlisting some trusted men to help you. They will likely see your blind spots. If they're worth their salt as friends, they'll call you out.

Often the answer to these questions is more subtle and involves areas within ourselves that we haven't fully probed. For example, the quality of our attention. Am I just being physically present? Do I lead when it's called for, or do I simply hand all responsibility of the decision-making to my feminine partner? Do I bring real empathy to the relationship and a "ride or die" spirit of devotion, or do I simply listen in a half-assed way when she speaks of her pain and desire? Do I create loving and conscious spaces for her to completely express the truth of her heart, or do I avoid her emotionality? Do I consistently foster sexual and relational energies that nourish and relax her? Again, I want to stress that you shouldn't take this as an opportunity to feel bad or shame yourself. Hardly any men were taught these gifts of leadership.

That being said, true personal responsibility requires us to constantly reflect on where we are withholding and falling short. Most men that come to me do so because they have a nagging feeling—sometimes even a profound knowing—that they have so much more to give.

Evoke (Don't Complain)

Right now, you have the capacity to change the thoughts, feelings, and actions of your feminine partner anytime you decide to. You can evoke the very best or worst in her simply through your way of being. You can affect and change her brain chemistry, as well as her hormones, simply by the way you breathe, ground, and move your own body. You can put tension in her body, or you can relax her nervous system with a touch or a breath. Your solid presence can evoke love energy in her, or your impatience and judgment can cause her mind to become reactive and her body to tighten. Your fierce desire can awaken energy in your exhausted partner's heart and genitals, or your tepid acknowledgment can be a pinprick to her heart.

The most profound and almost completely unrecognized truth of our relationships is that we are evoking from those around us all the time. Sometimes subtly, sometimes overtly. But our capacity to evoke states in the people we are near is truly one of the most powerful abilities we have as human beings. My millennial students call it a superpower.

This is the beautiful relational interdependence between all living things that too often goes unnoticed. This lack of awareness makes it possible for us to complain about not being met, seen, or respected by our partners—an epidemic in a world overrun with *me first* mentality. We will complain about what we don't get while simultaneously justifying why we can't give the love we know we are capable of giving to others, and little do we know that we could evoke something entirely different in our environments. Our willingness to give our bodies, hearts, and souls—*especially* when we don't want to—is the key to practicing spiritual intimacy and long, deep, artful loving. In fact, I believe it is the key to changing the collective consciousness on the planet.

The idea that our thoughts, feelings, and ways of being directly influence our physical surroundings has been studied and illustrated widely over the past several decades (most notably in the water experiments of Masaru Emoto). But the scientists involved are merely describing what yogis and mystics have known for millennia. Our intentional energy can either harm, heal, or transform other forms of consciousness. The sacred sounds of mantras change the energetic spaces in which they travel.

Chanting is shown to promote alpha or theta brainwaves associated with deep flow states. Slow breathing and intentional speech that emanates from the lower diaphragm have been shown to relax the nervous systems of those in proximity.

I have seen countless women whose heart-opened expressions of rage and grief brought the men in front of them to a stronger spine, clearer presence, and softer heart in a matter of seconds. I have seen women melt open when pierced with a strong slow breath and soft gaze. She was tense and closed a moment ago, and now her heart is free and her body soft. The only thing that changed was his unwavering presence and commitment to her.

So why don't we use our capacity to evoke the best in the people we love most? Because we have trained ourselves to withhold love. We certainly weren't born stingy; it developed over time and became a body-mind habit. Watch children or puppies play and it's obvious. The unfettered generosity and expressions of love that naturally flow from them cause us to smile and open automatically without thought or struggle or doubt.

Our reasons for withholding love are varied. We do it because we don't think we're being given the respect, presence, or energy we crave; we do it because we're too tired; we withhold because we're stressed, or because our parents trained us into believing that love was something to be earned. And so, when we give our devotion in an inspired moment and are not met with the response we think we should get, we close up, saying, "See? He's never interested in me" or "What's the point? She never responds to my affection." And the more we tell ourselves these things, the more we believe them, and we retreat further into our story about what real love looks like and doesn't.

PRACTICE THE GIFT OF OPENING

The next time you are standing in proximity to your feminine partner, consciously slow and extend your breath and feel the earth beneath your feet. Feel your core, your navel, your legs, and your genitals. Soften your heart and gaze with as much love—maybe even gratitude and awe—as you can muster in the moment. Let her feel your open-hearted and grounded presence fully taking her in. If you like, you can think something like, "I would do anything to keep you safe, to make you feel completely loved, and to ravish you into a melty puddle of bliss." Choose an intentional thought that expresses your most pure desire to give her your all. Notice how long it takes to get a positive response from her. A smile, a deep breath, a move toward you. Pay attention to your body and her body. It doesn't usually take more than a few minutes, and often less. I am constantly amazed at how easy it is to open the heart of another when we put our body-minds and some simple techniques to the test.

Hold the Pose

The solution to changing the trajectory of our destinies, receiving the best our lover has to offer, and feeling more fulfilled in love is simple. Rather than complain about what you aren't receiving, just focus instead on evoking the deepest, most powerful, and most fully expressed version of your feminine partner in that moment.

I'm about to offer some practices that, when taken on fully, can work in minutes if not seconds. But you must train yourself to *hold the pose*. Holding the pose means to continue to open through every impulse and instinct to close up, retreat, or give up. Similar to a challenging posture in a yoga sequence, holding the pose through the discomfort in a relationship is the only way to train your body and mind to stay in the fire—giving you the opportunity to burn through the often long-held body-mind habits of closure or retreat that keep you both stuck.

If you are craving her trust and surrender as a lover, how can you become—in your body, in this moment—the person she fully trusts with every inch of her heart and soul? As I described earlier, breathe more deeply. Steady your movements. Soften your heart. Make your gaze softer. Bring more playfulness until you can feel your partner's heart bloom. It isn't enough to sweetly nuzzle up after days of giving your mediocre presence and expect your feminine partner to be turned on. How committed are you? If it takes five minutes, ten minutes, or an hour to open her heart with your unrelenting love, are you willing to wait or take the time it requires for her to relax through the armor she's had to put on to survive? It might take longer than feels comfortable. Are you strong enough, open enough, and relaxed enough to stay with her through that discomfort? This is what it means to hold the pose. And just as we have all heard that the greatest gains come from the last few reps at the gym, it is in the moments of stretching and leaning just beyond what is habitually comfortable that your body and nervous system will gain the strength needed to go even deeper together.

3

THE POWER OF BREATH AND THE NEW CURRENCIES OF EMBODIMENT, PRESENCE, PLAY, AND INTEGRITY

THINK ABOUT YOUR breath, presence, capacity for playfulness, and integrity as invaluable currencies that bring richness, grounded comfort, and openness to your life and your relationships, especially your romantic ones. They are not extraneous luxuries that deserve half-hearted attention. They are commitments worth fighting for, especially if you want to be more trusted and attractive to the Feminine and the world at large. When you bring this kind of focus to cultivating these as assets, like a warrior willing to walk through a wall, it will empower incredible trust, love, and healing in every area of your life.

Breath and Embodiment

Breath is the first step in cultivating and maximizing the currencies mentioned above. Breath is the gateway to presence and relaxation. It clarifies wisdom and integrity in the moment, fosters nonreactivity, and promotes new possibilities when it comes to love and tussle. Full breathing can bring our parasympathetic nervous system online in times of stress, refreshing our sense of agency and heightening our emotional intelligence. How you breathe makes all the difference in how you experience your life, as well as how your life unfolds.

There is a way of breathing, standing, speaking, and gazing that will make any human, but especially men, feel more trustable to those around them. Most of us have not been taught the internal and external poses of embodied presence that would freely transmit the depth of who we truly are, but martial artists, monastics, and yogis have been teaching these skills for millennia. The problem is not your innate ability to bring a way of being that relaxes and inspires those you touch, but instead the habits of your unconscious body-mind that have taken hold over a lifetime.

It takes a disciplined physical, psychological, and energetic approach to unwind these karmic habits. The physical practices of strengthening and opening your body—when combined with a calm mind, profound breath, full relaxation, and a capacity to feel outward—create a state we call *presence*. And unbeknownst to a great number of us, it has become an incredibly valuable commodity, not only in intimate relationships but in the world at large. I would argue that in this distraction-driven and overwhelmed state of life, it is *the* most valuable commodity a human being can possess.

> The key to any transformative practice is in how it infuses and applies to your real-life experience.

Even so, too many of us have become unconscious to the one thing we actually can control: the transmission of our consciousness and depth through our body. As pandemics, politicians, and central banks seemingly upend our lives with impunity, a man's unwavering intention to presence and depth is a blessing to him and all of those around him. Women are awakening to this truth and are literally clamoring for it—calling in every possible way for men to cultivate this capacity.

Chances are—as you have sat still reading these words, for example—that you are completely unaware of your own breath. The resonance and power of the breath is the biological adamantine force that animates every minute of life, love, and all of reality. It is the contraction and expansion of all living things—all matter in the universe. This whole cosmic breath is right now breathing you as you are breathing it, and yet, breathing consciously is something that most people reserve exclusively for yoga or meditation. But the key to any transformative practice is in how it infuses and applies to your real-life experience, expanding your capacity and neurological patterns as you learn to apply newly developed skills in the moment.

Bridging our solo practices of consciousness, spirituality, and sensitivity into the most mundane, repetitive, and subtle experiences is the beginning of all yoga—physical, relational, and sexual. Breath is the fundament to these practices, ever deepening our infinite experience of any conscious moment. Whether that moment is spent ravishing your partner or paying your bills, breath makes all moments sacred. The more you practice breathing, the more you will be able to integrate the aliveness of your body-mind into the everyday household moments of your life. As your breath naturally deepens, your capacity to feel all of existence—from infinite consciousness to the most subtle shift of your lover's heartbeat—will increase.

And so, we will begin with the breath, its mechanisms and how it opens up our bioenergetic pathways to make us strong and increase our sensitivity, endurance, and fluidity. Life begins with a first breath, as does everything else, including sex, love, and healing. Wherever you are in your personal and relational life, your breath is the key to releasing stress and numbness. It unravels your grief and trauma, and it allows you to truly drop into what is happening in your experience. Returning to the breath is always the next right step.

I want to remind you again that this is all practice. Anytime we learn anything in the West, we have the compulsive need to do it right and be good at it (if not *the best*), and conscious breath practice is no different.

When we do something consciously that we would normally do unconsciously (such as breathing), it is an entirely different experience than doing something that we have never done before. You are *always* breathing, so when I introduce these breath practices, the meta-awareness of your breath might feel unfamiliar. The new mechanism of inhalation and exhalation will release the psycho-emotional patterns of habitual shallow breathing, and what might happen as a result is a feeling of clunkiness—like you cannot quite figure out *how* to breathe. This is totally normal and typically the result of unblocking channels within you that have sat constricted. Those closed channels are the storehouses of your psychological, physical, spiritual, and emotional blockages.

This is not the only reason I have dedicated an entire segment of this book to breath. It's also why I will continually remind you to be gentle with yourself as you learn. Beneath the breath rests the home of all of your numbness, trauma, lack of fulfillment, and pain. But also there lies the channels that will facilitate your deepest, most delicious, and most healing experiences of happiness, vitality, and intimacy.

For sexual yoga, I will focus on two specific breathwork practices that open and clear the central channel of the body. In some martial arts, this space is referred to as the *center line* and is the bundle of nerves and energetic meridians existing between your throat and perineum or cervix. David Deida also speaks about the importance of this channel as the deepest energetic and physical place in you. This breathwork serves to open the deepest, most sensitive parts of our anatomy—both physiological and energetic—from the inside out. This central column is the core of the central nervous system and empties directly into the genital area. Breathwork that specifically targets the lower abdomen and genitals—while connecting the heart and the throat through the central channel—is crucial if we want to energize the entire body and nervous system.

The second foundational breath practice I want to share with you is that of the relaxed, organic breath. Whereas the following Three-Part Breath practice is quite active (even exhaustive to some), the organic breath is one of complete relaxation into the exact rhythm of breath your body wants to take. There is no push, no forcefulness. There is only an awareness and surrender into the way your body wants to breathe—beyond practices that expand your capacity or everyday stresses that tense your body and limit your capacity to open in breath.

This is how true surrender, feeling, and openness become organic in your sexuality—through breath that strengthens and activates, followed by breath that relaxes and opens the body to the point of dropping you into your parasympathetic nervous system. Both are needed for the most profound intimacies. Of course, there are thousands of other pranayama, Taoist, or tantric practices out there, but these two will immediately strengthen, open, and relax your nervous system. If all you take from this book are these two breath practices into your life, I will be ecstatic. And your whole life will change. You are breathing an entirely new destiny into being.

PRACTICE **THREE-PART BREATH**

This is a foundational Taoist practice that employs breath to rewire your nervous system and increase your capacity to feel, relax, and energize your central channel and lower chakras. I highly recommend it as a daily practice. The more breath, openness, and relaxation you bring to these areas of your body, the more open, alive, and awake your feeling-body will become. The practice is also known to increase ejaculatory control.

The central column is also where we store most of our trauma, especially in the pelvic floor, solar plexus, and behind the heart. Like running water through a kinked garden hose, bringing breath to these areas frees the trauma and releases held-back emotions. This practice is also a simple way to connect your heart and sexual centers, opening them simultaneously. This is crucial, as heart-connected sex is the most healing and inspiring (and by far the sexiest).

You can practice the Three-Part Breath either on your back or in a comfortable upright seated position. Breathe fully into your belly so that it puffs out, then into the solar plexus located just below your ribs, and then into the upper chest. Exhale out the chest first, then the solar plexus, and finally, out of the belly, finishing with the belly falling in toward the spine. The idea is to fill every quadrant of your lungs as fully as possible and then release the air from the top down.

To break this down further, you can practice filling only the belly for several breaths, then only the solar plexus, and then only the upper chest before practicing putting them together. Once you become used to practicing this way, your breath will flow like a wave. For men, this will allow breath and life force to flow much more easily into your lower belly and genitals. It will increase your breath capacity and prepare your nervous system to hold more sexual and emotional energy. Your voice may drop—my voice did after a few months of doing it consistently. To strengthen ejaculatory control, practice this breath while masturbating or being touched by a partner. The idea is to use the breath to circulate the pleasure rather than letting it collect in the genitals prior to ejaculation. You will be much more capable of lasting longer in sex and will eventually be able to circulate the sexual energy not only through your body but through your partner's as well.

To practice with another person, both partners sit upright and cross-legged, facing one another, with knees gently touching, looking into one another's left eye (the receptive eye that is also the gateway to the right brain) and focusing on feeling into the depths of one another's heart. The masculine partner will begin Three-Part Breath, matching their rhythm to the feminine partner's breath, so they are not only breathing into their own belly, solar plexus, and chest but also energetically breathing into their feminine partner's. Then the masculine partner focuses on the feminine partner's central column, bringing awareness and breath to the channel between their throat and cervix. The feminine partner allows the masculine partner to match their breath. As the feminine partner breathes in, the masculine partner breathes them a little more deeply than she would breathe herself, as if opening her from the inside, and feeling her body soften with every breath. The masculine practice is to feel the feminine more thoroughly than she has ever been felt, while the feminine practice is to release control of her heart and nervous system to the masculine through breath and relaxation. As with so many of these practices, roles can and should be reversed whenever desired.

This is a practice of energetic attunement first taught to me by David Deida and is essential to cultivating the feeling awareness needed between lovers. Physical sex is great, but adding the polarizing and sensitizing nature of Three-Part Breath will take the depth of your connection to an entirely new level.

Being Present vs. Having Presence

The heart of what Deida has termed masculine spiritual practice accesses the space of infinite, unchanging awareness as witness to all that is happening, moving, and arising, moment to moment. Vipassana mindfulness—as well as the meditative tools of the Zen and Tibetan Buddhist traditions—are all helpful for anyone seeking to enhance their experience of stillness and the Infinite.

You can be in the present moment, or
you can be the present moment.

Unfortunately for many Westerners, this experience is too often disconnected from the body. As we become witness to our thoughts and emotions, feel into our consciousness, or connect to the empty space holding it all together, we may experience an expansive, alert, and ideally thoughtless state that many teachers describe as being *fully present*. For the Masculine in all of us, this state can be incredibly blissful. There is nothing to do and no one to impress. To be completely present to this moment and stretching out to infinity is a beautiful experience that anyone wanting to cultivate their spiritual Masculine could and should, in my opinion, practice daily.

This is not the same, however, as *having* presence. To have presence is an embodied meditative state that transmits a grounded, relaxed, full awareness of all that is. You can be *in* the present moment, or you can *be* the present moment. To embody presence means that the world will feel this width, stillness, depth, and openness—consciousness, if you will—*through your body*. It is one thing to rest and open up to the bliss of feeling consciousness; it is quite another to permeate a space or a moment with it pressed through our bodies and into the environment. To be the embodiment of conscious presence is the masculine gift to the Feminine and to the world. Sadly, few men take the time to cultivate it. To do so, we need breath, relaxation, body awareness, and openness. This is what separates the tantric or embodied practices of having presence, from the meditative practices of becoming present.

Tantra has many definitions, and the word is often misunderstood in the West. The simple definition I prefer is *to embody the divine*, and I think it's a serviceable translation in this context. For the purposes of my work, masculine development when it comes to tantra refers to the embodiment of consciousness—integrating awareness and feeling with our physical bodies. Your ability to do so is the most valuable, magnetic gift you can bring to all of your relationships.

Here's a straightforward practice for developing embodied presence. At first, it might come across as complicated to put together—somewhat like learning to drive a manual transmission vehicle for the first time. Like driving a stick, it gets easier with practice.

PRACTICE **EMBODIED PRESENCE**

Stand with your legs hip-width apart, feet pointing straight ahead as if on train tracks. Slightly tuck your chin, soften your gaze, and hold your arms out at the sides slightly— as if you were holding luggage—but with your fingers and hands relaxed. Your breath should be slow and steady through your nose, tongue placed gently on the roof of your mouth. Allow your legs to become heavy and grounded, as if they could sink a foot into the earth. Invite the earth to infuse your legs with its natural flow of energy. Focus on the sensations in your legs, becoming more and more aware of the weight of gravity pulling them down into the earth.

Once you begin to experience a sense of groundedness, bring your awareness to your belly and breathe as deeply as you can. Allow your abdomen to rise and fall with each breath. Feel the air passing through your throat, past the back of your heart, and into your abdomen. Continue for at least two minutes until your body begins to feel more alive.

Next, relax the muscles around your heart and bring your awareness to the powerful flow of life that moves through it. Spend a few moments surrendering any tightness in your heart, imagining it softening and blooming open like a rose. Soften the muscles behind your eyes, too—this will help your heart relax.

Then, with a grounded posture and your body alive with breath and an open heart, bring your mind's eye inward to the unchanging you. Feel for a beginning or an end to the inner cosmos of your infinite consciousness. Find the vast part of you that never changes and never ends. Do this without losing the awareness of a grounded and alive body.

Now put all of these elements together in a dynamic meditation—legs grounded, belly full of the life force of breath, heart relaxed and open, body-mind awareness resting as infinite consciousness. Amplify each trait, as if you could fill every cell of your body and, eventually, the room with their textures. Be sure to scan your body for any tension and let each exhalation relax you even more. The end result will be a full, relaxed, grounded, heart-opened, and conscious presence that will have a very particular impact on anyone in front of you (especially a sexual partner).

This practice will help you learn what it means to have presence. Learning to do it unflinchingly is the masculine challenge.

Masculine Integrity in Relationship

Most men see the concept of integrity as a challenging and sometimes overwhelming standard of living they will never attain. Many see it as a burden. And because the Masculine is always looking for completion, integrity as a practice is rarely undertaken. I prefer to look at integrity as an ever-expanding commitment to meticulous awareness—a dynamic meditation that is never mastered but always gestured toward.

Men often get tripped up on thinking of integrity as the same thing as keeping one's word, or they moralize integrity unnecessarily. I think a more useful way to approach integrity as the masculine partner in any relationship is to contemplate and apply this definition: *Integrity is the state of whole and complete soundness—undiminished and unimpaired.*

If you're the primary masculine partner and you want to experience profound trust and sexual depth with your partner, then you are responsible for the foundational soundness and wholeness of the relational field. Just as if you owned a business or were building a beautiful building or structure, the whole thing would fall apart without soundness and wholeness. Of course, that doesn't mean that your partner's Masculine side won't share in the responsibility of maintaining what I would call the *devotional integrity* between you. But it must be primarily your charge to guard and cultivate it if you want her to relax and bring her energy and love to the dance.

Any masculine partner can do this by first surveying the foundation, field, and structure of the relationship with feeling awareness and keen insight. What feels wobbly? What is strained? Is there a lack of honest sharing? Are one or both partners exhausted and malnourished? Is there bitterness and unresolved resentment? Is the sexual intimacy predictable or shallow? There are hundreds of aspects for your awareness to consider. The capacity to be conscious of the cracks and fissures in the relationship and then attend to them diligently is an incredible gift the Masculine brings to the art of sexual and relational intimacy. Of course, the same practice can be applied to your business, mission, or role as a parent.

Once the structurally unsound areas of your love dynamic are identified, consider what needs to be addressed. For example, if the soundness of your love is diminished by the shallow or infrequent nature of your sex, then your commitment to integrity compels you to look into changing that. If there is bitterness, resentment, judgments, or projections that weaken the integrity of your commitment to each other, how can those be cleared compassionately and openly? If one of you has unprocessed trauma that is causing damage to your relationship, it is up to you to look into healing it, whether with psychotherapy or other modalities. Your integrity in relationship, especially in love, requires you to have your eyes, heart, and feeling body wide open. That's what it takes to identify your structural weaknesses and amplify your strengths.

It's not as difficult as you might think. And the incredible self-esteem, devotion, and trust that can follow shouldn't be understated. Of course, some of the necessary conversations with your lover can and will be difficult, and it will take guts to make stands for the strength of your relationship. But that is what she will love in the end. As long as she can feel the depth of your pledge to hold you both to the best you can bring, she will respect and appreciate whatever challenges are required to elevate your relationship.

> Most men falsely apply the logic that their feminine partner should be just as responsible for practicing integrity and self-awareness as they are.

And remember, she is carrying the pain of her personal story in her body and nervous system, as well as the pain that millions of women have suffered from the lack of masculine integrity. In the end, your meticulous integrity can help heal that—a balm to her nervous system, and perhaps one she never knew was missing.

Masculine vs. Feminine Integrity

One of the more common complaints I get from men goes like this: "Look, I'm doing so much to try to be a better man, but she still dumps her unprocessed and unfiltered emotions on me without owning her part at all. Why shouldn't she be accountable, too? Are you telling me I should just hold space while she's raging and dumping on me?"

This points to a larger area of confusion for most masculine partners. To put it simply, it's a mistake to assume that the Feminine values what the Masculine does. Most men falsely apply the logic that their feminine partner should be just as responsible for practicing integrity and self-awareness as they are. When she doesn't, they use their unmet expectations to justify disconnecting or, worse, bailing out of the relationship with the age-old idea that they tried everything possible, so therefore she just wasn't the *right woman*.

Granted, her Masculine side is responsible for integrity and self-awareness. That being said, her Feminine is not. And so, if you, like most masculine-identified men, are interested in leading a sexually polarized relationship in which your partner fully trusts your integrity and reveals her body, soul, and heart to you (much, if not most of the time), then you cannot expect her Feminine to act in the same way as your Masculine. It's a kind of torture I often see men inflict upon themselves and their partners, and it regularly leaves women completely confused as they try to contort themselves into what men say they want.

As David Deida beautifully describes in his teachings on Feminine responsiveness, the romantic partner who is primarily identified with the Feminine is not concerned with the details of events, or long-held values, or the consistency of an argument or position. For the Feminine—and remember that this is as true for a man in his Feminine as well—truth is what *feels* true for the optimal flow of love and self-expression in the moment. It is not a detail that happened or a promise that was made. It is not a logical conclusion based on past behaviors or facts. This relationship to truth is crazy-making for many masculine-centered people, but completely natural for someone in their Feminine. For the feminine essence—fully connected to the flow of love that is the core of who she is—truth has everything to do with the love, depth, and consciousness from you that she can both detect and trust.

For the purposes of our exploration, however, it's important to understand that the maintenance of this texture of truth *is* the Feminine responsibility in relationship. She is meant to bring you back to embodied consciousness through a moment-by-moment revelation of her heart. She is responsible for being the weathervane of the dynamic between you. Her precision is measured by revealing—day to day and moment to moment—how much love is flowing, how conscious you are, and how well you are leading the relationship, yourself, and your family. Are you navigating her into the ever-deeper chambers of her heart? How connected are you to your children? How skillful are you navigating the contours of work-life stress, technology, nourishment, and play in your lives? Her responsibility is to be a kind of intuitive oracle, guiding you back to presence, depth, and open-heartedness in all of these areas, all of the time.

If you are drifting into numbing activities or self-centered reflection, indulging in neurotic thought loops, or just completely oblivious to her need for connection, her sacred obligation is to share how it affects her body and heart. She is your lighthouse when you are drifting or lost. This is her primary gift to you and one of her greatest values. Think of it as an alarm bell for both your level of integrity and consciousness in the moment and in your life in general. She is meant to snap you into the present moment by letting you know when you are disembodied, untrustable, or just full of shit. Of course, she can always develop more artful means of doing this—preferably in ways you can metabolize. This doesn't mean she has free rein to criticize and complain, but it does indicate that she is responsible for showing how painful it is when the man she loves checks out, loses awareness, or drifts.

What lies beneath her complaints—once you truly pay attention—is a roadmap that leads you back to the present moment. My partner once pounded her fists on my chest and yelled, with tears in her eyes, "Come back to me, asshole! I'm right here!" It woke me up immediately. The complication is that many women were not taught how to energize the relationship from this place, just as most men weren't taught the power of loving, embodied presence. For this reason, she will sometimes end up in the swamp of broken-heartedness—a sort of enraged muteness—unable to share with you the pain she is experiencing, without you raging back, collapsing, or leaving altogether. This surfaces most often as nagging, complaining, or closing herself off in passive-aggressive ways.

This is where your depth of awareness, wisdom, and commitment to love come in. Rather than expecting her to jump into the logical, integral space of her own Masculine in the middle of a dispute, deftly guide her to a place where both of you can reflect on how your dynamic has gone astray.

If you feel she is not coming from the most sacred place within her or that she is relating from a neurosis or some unknown shadow that she is projecting onto you, then you have to create a container to bring her back. If she is disembodied—disconnected from the flow of love that is her essence—and coming at you with a closed heart, or if she isn't taking responsibility for her unowned rage and grief birthed years before you arrived on the scene, or if she is continuously telling you that you're wrong for what you think and feel, then you have to provide her with the tools of practice and model them for her *if you want her to stay in her Feminine*.

The good news is that it's easier than most people think. It just takes some creativity and an understanding of how each of you need to own your individual truths. Become a scientist of the energetic flow that is always pulsing between you, and learn to be an artist of communication techniques in service of love.

There are hundreds of practices you could do to help create a culture of self-reflection in both of you: "Let's each name three ways that we are making each other unfairly wrong," for example, or "Let's take three minutes each to share how we worship and punish each other." The point is that if you both crave a sexually polarized relationship above all else, then it is the masculine partner's responsibility to create these containers and lead the relationship back to open-hearted connection.

This works in reverse, as well. You may be squarely in your Feminine, overwhelmed by a sense of confusion as to why there isn't more love flowing or how to change it. You might have completely forgotten a promise or agreement you made and are unable to own your own slippage through your pain. You may be blaming her or projecting your fears and doubts about the relationship on her. And when the tables turn like this (which they will from time to time), if you have modeled well or if she has learned on her own, she may lead you both back to clarity on how your neuroses may be creating the rift in your connection.

Please remember that this concept isn't gender-based. It's about cultivating a clarity as to who should hold the most meticulous awareness in any moment and what is needed to reestablish trust for love to flow. In a sacred romance, both partners share a profound commitment to generously and skillfully guiding each other to the truest places of who they essentially are. So, to reiterate: if you are primarily masculine, your essence is consciousness; if your partner is primarily feminine, their essence is love. Integrity in the relationship has to reflect these truths.

The Art of the Tussle

The capacity to bring playfulness and humor to a relationship is one of the most potent currencies you have at your disposal. Humor is still commonly identified as one the sexiest traits a masculine-identified person can bring to his love life. It disarms tensions, pokes fun at habitual stories, and makes art out of sensitive wounds. Playfulness and humor, specifically in the context of sexual intimacy, is what Deida refers to in his book *Blue Truth* as "tussle," or "flowery combat."

This is quite different from the goofy exchanges I see too many couples fall into. Childish play and relating is all fine and good, but it rarely does much to spark erotic tension. In contrast, *tussle* is the practice of using humor, physicality, playful challenge, and even cockiness to create erotic tension between you. Tussle is consciousness expressed through play. It falls into the "high risk, high reward" domain of relational practice, but it's more than worth it. Tussle communicates your ability to stay open and playful in the midst of her criticism or moodiness, and, when done right, becomes a powerful form of foreplay that says, "Give me your best, I know how to handle you, my love." One beautiful aspect of tussle is that its primary intention is to open her heart, especially when she is in a shit mood or upset with you about something. It's not meant to mock or belittle her in any way, nor is tussle use simply to make her laugh (although that has its place in any romance).

Tussle can instantly wipe out previous moments of unconsciousness or bitterness in favor of love's joyful expression. It can take the form of you pulling her close and kissing her neck while saying, "I love it when you call me an asshole." Or it can be as simple as a wry smile at a snide comment. It can be offering your arm up for her to punch when you have been a jerk. No matter what form it takes, the whole point of tussle is to move energy with her. And the more Feminine in nature your partner is, the more energy will need to be moved. Tussle is a conscious and open leaning into what is moving through her body, while also being committed to the playful flow or sexual tension that keeps your relationship juicy.

Now, of course you will need the wisdom and sensitivity to discern when she is truly upset and needs your complete presence and support. But it's just as important to know when she just has energy she needs to move with you. So many men mistake the latter for the former and end up overprocessing or bringing too much seriousness to an issue in an effort to get to the bottom of things.

Remember, the Feminine in all of us is interested in the flow and exchange of love at all times. That doesn't mean she needs her moods dissected. Sometimes it's just rainy or windy in her heart, and how you interact with her in those moments will set the tone of your relating for days, weeks, or much longer. So, developing the skill—and it is a skill—to unabashedly, spontaneously, and boldly express love's play is a tremendous gift. I would go so far as to say tussle is an invaluable nutrient for her nervous system. It is a need for her—not just a frivolous desire. Without it, love withers in her body and she will long for someone or something that can free her heart with confidence, play, and depth.

STRENGTHEN YOUR NERVOUS SYSTEM

Train Your Nervous System

Training yourself to lead in all areas of your life will require more than physical strength and emotional fortitude. It will require a fluid and adaptable nervous system as well. There is nothing wrong with physical strength and mental toughness, but they don't necessarily lead to the most steadfast emotional capacity, nor do they in and of themselves transmit clarity and integrity to those around us. Creating trust, inspiration, and relaxation will require a powerful nervous system that allows you to remain open in challenging circumstances. After all, this is when and where our openness and heart-centered leadership are most needed — in the difficult conversations, uphill battles, and moments in which inspiration and love are most craved by the people we love.

Openness is at once a spiritual, physical, and emotional experience. It requires a simultaneous relaxation of our minds into the Infinite — widening our corporal and energetic bodies and revealing our deepest emotional truths. When we activate these states together at a consistently high level, we transmit a more profound state of openness others can feel and trust, but this transmission takes work.

At the heart of all of this is our nervous system. Its tentacles, preganglionic neurons, electric currents, dendrites, and neurotransmitters stimulate and connect our spiritual, physical, and emotional bodies in ways we still barely understand. The part of you that can relax into receiving strong feedback from your partner or stay open and loving during a fight is the by-product of a strong nervous system. Your ability to override fight-or-flight impulses will dictate much in the realm of success for you. Martial artists and yogic masters have known this for millennia, and Western wellness modalities are beginning to embrace this truth as well.

Suffice to say, without a strong nervous system, we cannot sustain relaxed openness for very long. The habits of closure that were long ago installed into our body-minds are too well grooved. But as we practice strengthening our bodies, hearts, and minds beyond our consciously driven sympathetic nervous systems and into the latent wisdom of our parasympathetic ones, our ways of being naturally elevate. We become wiser, more relaxed and open, less thought-driven, and increasingly heart connected. We enter a flow state. And our capacity to love, fuck, lead, and feel go through the roof.

These superior ways of being—as well as the psycho-physio shifts they induce—are not possible unless you develop a nervous system capacity to *hold the pose and relax* beyond what you find comfortable. That means developing an inner core strength that allows your comfort zone to expand dramatically. This is what Dan Siegel refers to as the *window of tolerance*. In this zone, your body can hold more energy—both yours and others—and it's also where karmic change, sublime connection, and profound inspiration exist. For example, your capacity to withstand and hold a feminine storm of emotion—especially if directed at you—and then powerfully choose a path to lead is directly linked to your nervous system's capacity to hold energy. Your ability to metabolize massive amounts of sexual energy, reveal a vulnerable emotion, or hold a screaming child with a relaxed heart requires the same kind of solidity. Even your capacity to lead a contentious board meeting with grace and calm is a by-product of your nervous system strength.

> Natural wisdom, strength, and calm can flow
> confidently—regardless of what life throws your way.

The simple truth is our nervous systems hold the key to most everything we desire. Very few people understand this, unfortunately, and so we regularly turn away from what is challenging, usually by engaging one lesser distraction or another. Even worse, we fail to recognize that our fragile and overwhelmed nervous systems unconsciously guide us to do so.

Nervous system training has at its core a combination of physical challenge, breath awareness, emotional openness, and energetic relaxation—often for sustained periods of time. Iron shirt qigong, for example, may require a practitioner to hold a pose in relative stillness and full breath for many minutes. But the true goal isn't simply to hold the pose or gain strength; it's to remain calm, open, and aware while doing so. At the height of the discomfort, the practitioner may be directed to expand awareness outward to the immediate environment or beyond (rather than inward, as most humans do under stress). The impact of conditioning the body-mind to remain wide in equanimity while encountering strong emotions will allow you to stay tethered to consciousness through the body rather than become ungrounded or, worse, unhinged in the face of chaos. From this place, natural wisdom, strength, and calm can flow confidently—regardless of what life throws your way.

Ground Your Body and Widen Your Awareness

One of the core benefits of grounding and strengthening your nervous system is that you gain the capacity to maintain an unbound and free consciousness in challenging situations. This is one of the key attributes I learned from my teachers in regard to masculine value. Rather than collapse into habitual, often self-centered thought when faced with one of life's storms—from your partner, your work, or the world in general—expand your feeling awareness outward into the field you want to impact and make calm, thoughtful choices that will serve you and those around you.

This capacity starts with grounding, which is the breath and awareness practice of plugging your body—especially your lower body—into the energetic field of the earth. It's not as esoteric as it might sound. Simply setting the intention to connect your nervous system to the magnetic field of the earth and pressing your body awareness downward will transform how you feel internally and how others experience you. Your thoughts will slow, your breath will likely deepen, your parasympathetic nervous system comes more online, and those around you will feel more at ease.

I've seen this play out countless times in my workshops. As masculine partners connect their bodies and awareness to the rock, soil, and energy of the planet, their feminine partners soften and relax, trusting them more. It's a gift to be grounded and then ground others from that place—be it a child, lover, or a room of strangers.

PRACTICE **GROUNDING AND EXPANDING**

Start with a strong standing pose. Open the soles of your feet and imagine they are sunk six inches into the ground. Then imagine your navel and genitals are pressed into the terra firma beneath. You can even practice expanding the feeling awareness down to the earth's core, eventually learning to connect the sacrum, spine, and root of your heart downward—thousands of feet into the earth.

Once you have learned how to ground yourself fully, let your awareness widen. Across the room, the neighborhood, the land, the planet. Feel outward into the forests, deserts, and oceans. Let yourself become attuned to the massive sources of life around you. It will provide energy and inspiration to the moment. Imagine placing yourself in the center of the most pristine forest or hundreds of feet down in the blue ocean and notice what happens inside your nervous system. You will likely feel an alert peacefulness that both inspires and expands you.

Once you have practiced grounding your body and widening your awareness, you can begin to add practices and postures that will create strength while you maintain this grounded width. The more you practice, the more your nervous system will be able to stabilize and relax while you take in more and more life. Again, this is an art that your body can master and one that will allow you to take in more of your feminine partner, your children, your environment, and your community.

PRACTICE STRENGTHENING YOUR NERVOUS SYSTEM

Drop into a horse stance. Your legs should be about one foot wider than your hips, with your feet turned outward at sixty degrees. Squat at least six inches down, pulling your navel in slightly while imagining pressing your sacrum and spine into the earth. Bring attention to the center column of your body in front of your spine and root that into the earth as well.

Inhale through your nose and exhale through pursed lips, like a whistle without sound. Place your arms out, about heart level, as if you were hugging a tree or beach ball. Keep your fingertips about four inches apart and your arms and shoulders relaxed, but make sure your legs, core, and spine are strong. Continue to breathe in this manner throughout the pose.

As the sensation in your body increases, keep your breath and body as relaxed as possible without dropping the pose. Keep some of your awareness on the center column in your body and some of your awareness on the environment around you. Start with the room or space around you and keep pressing your awareness outward, like a sonar wave. Pay special attention to your heart, allowing it to relax into the width of your arms, and even beyond.

Start with five minutes of this practice and build your way up to twenty. The goal is relaxation, wide awareness, and fluid breath throughout. If you can't continue the breath as outlined, just relax the pose slightly. With practice, your ability and sensation will expand.

PRIORITIZE DEPTH OVER COMFORT

The Magnetism of Depth

The more completely you bring your breath, awareness, and sensitivity into the core of your emotional, physical, or spiritual body, the more magnetic and attractive you will become. If you can master focusing your awareness on the core spaces of your heart, lower abdomen, and central column of your body, you will be felt as more still, more relaxed, more confident, and ultimately more attractive to others. I have watched this play out in workshop after workshop, over twelve years and with hundreds of participants. Those in their Feminine clearly respond, spontaneously, to the exact moments the Masculine brings his awareness and sensitivity to his physical or emotional depth, be it the core of his core heart, his pelvic floor, the most tender spot of his emotional body, or his central column that runs from his perineum to his throat.

If you cultivate the capacity to drop into your core emotional truth at any moment, you will be unshakeable in your authenticity, and others will feel it. If you can train your mind's eye toward the unchanging center of your inner self, you will create a tether to consciousness, and your nervous system will transmit the still essence of that awareness through your body. People will feel the spaciousness of your inner understanding and be drawn to you.

The practices I'm offering here have the power to bring you more fully into the personal, relational, and spiritual essence of every moment.

PRACTICE CONTACTING THE CORE

Expand your breath down into your pelvic floor—at the base of your abdomen. Breathe fully, enough that the pelvic floor presses down into your genitals and your belly expands. Next, place all of your awareness on the sensations of your pelvic floor, abdomen, and genitals. Go into these spaces as they open and expand.

Now, without losing this awareness, feel into the bottom of your heart. Allow the texture of what is true there to arise. Notice its nature and characteristics—anxiety, love, fierceness, commitment, and so on. Next, ground it into the bottom of your heart without losing the breath and pelvic floor awareness you cultivated a minute ago. You have just deepened more fully into the core of your heart.

You should be able to feel your nervous system slow down and ground. You will likely have a more complete sense of the moment. You can, of course, expand this meditative practice ad infinitum to include all phenomena within and around you. Feeling more into the energy of the space immediately around you, your spine, your desires, the infinite expanse of space, the hearts of others . . . there is no end to this practice. Like so much of this work, it is a never-ending gesture into the truest nature of all things—as felt and expressed through your body.

The more you make this your home base, the more you will open, relax, and inspire those around you. The more people will seek you out. The more women will trust you with their hearts. The more money people will want to pay you.

There aren't studies to prove this is true and no scientific paper (that I know of) verifies the connection between depth and magnetism, yet I have seen it work with thousands of people over the years. Try these practices and find out for yourself.

Prioritize Depth Over Comfort

Depth occurs when we seek to go underneath the surface sensation, emotion, or tendency and into the core essence of something. There are always textures, truths, and essences beneath the surface of our emotions, our sex, or our environments. We can attune to them at any moment, feeling into the root of a difficult emotion, the base of our heart, or the present moment, for example. Revealing the parts of you that you may want to hide — or connecting to the source of a flower in bloom — requires intention, focus, and feeling. The by-product of doing so is peace, openness, and radical aliveness.

> We are fed relentless cultural messaging that satisfaction is the by-product of winning and accumulating.

Comfort, in contrast to depth, primarily is about creating or sustaining pleasure. It causes settling in the body and nervous system rather than expansion and growth. I'm referring to the comfort of daily routines, the comfort of settling for what is familiar in sex, or the comfort of holding back your truth to avoid conflict or of shying away from making a bold request. These things lead us as men, little by little, to become dull and flaccid. The process is almost imperceptible, but over time our nervous systems begin to seek more and more comfort. And we soften and become increasingly numb.

It's not your fault. Most men, unless they had extraordinary fathers, were not taught the power of doing otherwise. Over the past century, particularly since the 1950s, men were taught to prioritize comfort, particularly by becoming ardent consumers. We've been taught to make as much money as possible so that we can accumulate as much material wealth and freedom as we can in order to be safe and comfortable for the rest of our lives. That's the retirement paradigm, at least—comfortable house, comfortable lifestyle, lots of toys, retire in peace.

Comfort has become a bit of an addiction in the Western world, but I particularly see it at work in men. It's men who are taught to win, to play, and to accumulate. Again, not that creating a life of comfort is wrong in some way, but when the rituals of manhood have been by and large forgotten and in their place we are fed relentless cultural messaging that satisfaction is the by-product of winning and accumulating, we are headed in the wrong direction. And most of us know it.

Throughout the centuries around the world, men were given practices to seek out challenges, cultivate their hearts, and live with discomfort. Often these rituals involved facing physical, emotional, or egoic death—on a hunt or in a formal practice of manhood. Some people in the Sioux Nation still practice the Sundance ritual, chests pierced with cordage and hanging from a tree for days on end in order to face death and enhance their connection to the Great Mystery. Certain martial arts, meditative traditions, and yogic lineages require practices that demand extended, pristine awareness while holding physical poses that most people would deem impossible.

By and large, Westerners have lost these rituals. Instead, the men of today are taught to win through innovation, extraneous physical prowess, ruthlessness, and business acumen—not by feeling more fully into the moment and relaxing completely.

This is where men's work comes in. If done correctly, men's work will help a man seek out the areas where he is prioritizing comfort over his own depth and growth, and challenge him to expand. And, of course, these challenges do not have to be physical or self-mutilative in nature. Some men hold back their gifts and messages to the world because they are terrified to speak in public. Maybe their challenge would be to stand on a park bench and deliver their sermon to passers-by. Or perhaps a man avoids his fear of death at all costs. His medicine might be to envision the moment of his death and allow it to unfold without turning away. Or maybe he withholds core vulnerabilities from his lover out of fear she will reject him. He might be given a practice to share what he is most afraid for her to know about him. Suppose a man dropped a meditative pose at the first sign of physical discomfort. His group of men might challenge him to hold the pose while taking his awareness in his core and relaxing open.

In meeting these challenges, men gain confidence, solidity, and aliveness. All of these examples are ways to press a man into his edge (or slightly beyond) and teach him to relax his nervous system into the stretch—giving him an internal strength that can't be created by mere exercise.

What makes these practices different from simple physical challenges is their purpose—to uncover the habitual resistances in your life. These resistances then become the practice. They are gateways to a more profound understanding of yourself, your world, and maybe even the infinite nature of existence. They require a consistent reaching beyond your comfort zone, a constant awareness of how you are prioritizing the easy over the more challenging yet rewarding approach. This is where a group of men who can challenge your assumptions will be invaluable. I'll speak more about men's work later on, but for now I'll just share this short anecdote.

I was sitting in a cave a half-mile underground in the middle of January in the pre-dawn hours. I was instructed to stare at a wall between two candles for eight hours. My teacher at the time told me to sit there until I had a vision of what was most important for me to address in my life. I would have much rather discussed the matter back at the warm hotel in Sedona, Arizona. Lucky for me, he knew that cave would be more conducive to the journey I had to make. What eventually came to me in that bone-chilling, dark, and uncomfortable cave was a very personal message about my father and our healing, and it was a message I never would have received had I simply talked about what I thought I needed to do about the relationship. What I experienced couldn't happen in comfort.

Finding True Freedom

While the primary feminine complaint usually has to do with the myth of not enough love, the core masculine complaint involves the burden of responsibility. In fact, the weight of responsibilities are usually what men blame for their lack of availability to their intimate partners. More often than not, however, it's not so much the amount of work a man has on his plate that's behind the habitual closure, but his relationship to it. The myth he suffers from tells him that freedom is possible, but only *when* such-and-such happens down the road to alleviate his burdens—more money, less debt, a graduating child, a less demanding partner. Men (myself included) are subject to believing in these alluring delusions.

The truth is that complaining about our burdens—actual or imaginary—doesn't serve us as much as fully feeling the place within us that aches for freedom. Most men I know feel a profound pain around not being able to experience true freedom, and many of them don't even know that this is what's behind their hopelessness and inability to be present in the moment. They will point to the surface-level problem of being overly busy while ignoring the yearning at the core. I believe this is why so many men are suffering from depression, anxiety, and substance abuse. Not because something is wrong with them, but because they are not truly willing to face the ache in their hearts they have for real freedom.

Instead, they just pile on more shit to do, or they make endless lifestyle changes, thinking that completing some task or hitting some fundamentally arbitrary goal is going to liberate their hearts and souls. They will swallow whatever pill is meant to convince them that achievement equals freedom (or perhaps it's traveling the world or sexual liberation). Well, as any of us who have achieved substantial goals in life or have traveled extensively or have had multiple sexual partners will tell you— those experiences won't do it. They're nice in their own way, but they're not going to set you free.

Let Her Appear

Men regularly ask me how to attract the right romantic partner. They are often not very clear on what that means; they just have a sense that there is more available in the realms of sex, love, and devotion than they've experienced.

What they actually want to know is how to bring a feminine partner into their world who will want to reveal all of herself, who won't hold back, who will offer the range of Feminine experience—her fierce feedback, her darkest fantasies, her most tender fears, and her unwavering devotion. How can they attract someone like that? Someone to bring them warmth and sunlight, someone to inspire them to create something powerful in the world, and—most importantly—someone to unveil the nature of all existence through her sex and her body. And if they're already in a committed relationship with someone they love, men want to know how to evoke all of the above and more.

> Find where life is begging you to drop in more
> and face it with unwavering abandon.

Not surprisingly, the answer isn't what most men expect. But here it is: if you want to attract a devoted partner who will bless you with their radiance and fullness, then you must become who you are meant to be first. This could happen inside or outside of a relationship. What matters is that you must determine what is most crucial for you in life and then go for it. Whether it regards your body, mind, or spirit, you have to create a space and practice that access your innate potency and expand your capacities. That could mean joining a men's group, devoting yourself to martial arts, diving into a crucial mission, or committing to a meditation practice. Whatever it is, you need to commit fully to the purpose and lifestyle you know is burning inside of you and then craft a way of living in which you have no choice but to give everything to it.

If your life is uninspiring, you have to create whatever plan is going to encourage you to become lit up by your own existence and opportunities. If you wrestle with addictions or past demons, then dive in and face them squarely. If you are regularly malnourished by your lack of capacity to find peace and beauty in the world, it's on you to commit to activities that replenish your soul—unapologetically. Is there some heart-wrenching grief you need to heal? Go all in and feel it.

Whatever it is, find where life is begging you to drop in more and face it with unwavering abandon. Let go of the seeking and grasping for feminine approval or energy. Don't keep numbing out on the comfort and distractions all around you and expect a feminine being of pristine heart to find you attractive, because she won't. Or if she's already in your life, don't expect her to trust you with anything truly life changing.

On the other hand, if you do show the discipline, courage, and strength to take care of these issues, you will become more magnetic than you ever imagined. The Feminine and the world will not be able to ignore your depth, and incredible opportunities and people will start to appear in your life. Women you once believed out of your league will notice your presence and unwavering commitment to your own integrity, and these are qualities potential partners value that have very little to do with looks and bank accounts.

Make it a priority to learn to widen your awareness beyond your schemes, desires, and grasping for success. Train your mind to feel beyond the habitual thoughts of the current moment, the current burden, or the current annoyance. Let yourself expand into the infinite nature of existence and see what it does to your heart, mind, and body, as well as the nervous systems of those around you. Become the space of consciousness, holding all that you see, feel, and experience. Most often this can take the form of the dynamic meditation work I offer here, but it doesn't need to be formal.

As you master these practices, notice the people who float into your life. As they do, let them know how special they are. If they inspire you, say, "Your heart is inspiring," or "I can feel how much you love," or "Jesus, you're beautiful," and see how they respond. Tell her you'd like to know her better, always speaking from your depth and intimate relationship with the Infinite. Trust the magnetic beauty of your heart and purpose in the world. There's someone out there (or several someones) who wants to give you everything. You simply have to deepen and widen enough to receive it.

PRACTICE WIDENING AWARENESS

Start in an easy but alert seated position. Deepen your breathing and spread your awareness 360 degrees outward. Feel your neighborhood, the city around you, and the countryside that surrounds the city. Pay special attention to how much life is happening around you in this very moment—whether it be people or nature or traffic. When you walk down the street, feel the whole street. Feel the people around you. Feel everything in the environment.

When you walk into a room, try removing the focus from yourself and placing it on the shape and texture of the room. As you develop this capacity, you become more trustworthy as a man, a leader, a visionary, and a lover. The Feminine will consider you to be someone they can open to fully. So, relax past any habitual self-referential thinking and become a man who can feel out into the cosmos, eventually allowing the Infinite to be felt through his gaze. Other people, especially women, can sense when you do this. In fact, they crave it. They are seeking a man who has a profound relationship with the Infinite and can share it with them.

Clarify Your Core Truths

You must continually reevaluate what is most true for you and then take complete ownership of aligning your life with it. Anything less and you will feel chronically off. Your romantic partner will not be able to fully trust you, and the world will sense that you are living out of step with your own personal integrity.

This means you must remove as much distraction and responsibility as possible and sit quietly with the reality and direction of your mission on the planet, your intimate relationships, and your personal expression of who you truly are. What was true last year isn't necessarily who you are now (although it could be). Most of us blindly charge forward like tanks without investigating our internal and external environments, which is how far too many of us waste precious time on matters that have very little to do with our core truths.

Our unconscious impulses to marry a certain person or head down a specific career path often have more to do with societal pressures, our family of origin, or even traumas passed down from our ancestors. I remember sitting on my great aunt's lap as a seven-year-old and her telling me, with tremendous love and affection, that the best thing a man could do in life was to earn a PhD (like my cousin Mark) and become a teacher. This memory came back to me when I was twenty-nine and working on my doctorate at New York University. She was right about becoming a teacher, it's just that I wasn't meant to take an academic path to do so, and it took me years to figure that out. A lot didn't work out the way I wanted it to, but every twist and turn along the way was necessary to get to where I am now. Even so, I wonder what it would have been like to have had the tools I have now when I was younger. In part, that's what I hope to offer you in this book.

Whatever path lies ahead for you, it will serve you to enhance your awareness and constantly clarify your core truths. Over time, you will attune to them. With practice, you will more intuitively know how consciousness—the great reality of life—wants to express itself through you, moment by moment. Along the way, use the men in your life to get feedback on how trustable you are in your reflections. Building intuitive muscle takes time, and masculine beings can be prone to impulsive decisions. But having other trustworthy men involved in your process will hold you in a place of sharp reflection that you would likely not be able to achieve alone.

Once you have honed your capacity to recognize and feel into the center of your own heart, you can begin to bring this feeling awareness to the more immediate and everyday decisions you face. What needs to be prioritized this week? What do I need most to feel nourished and alive today? What does my romantic relationship most need to be juicy and thrive? What would most benefit my children? Remember, your most profound masculine gift is your pristine awareness. Taking on practices, situations, and teachers to sharpen and refine it will inform you and those around you that you are a man of truth and integrity, as well as someone who can be trusted in this life.

One practice I learned from David Deida was to ask one question every day: What do I need to do so that I can put my head down on the pillow tonight without any thought? In other words, what do I need to do in order to die with a sense of completion? I will offer a version of this practice later in the book, but for now just consider the question. For me, it's almost always just a couple of things that I have to attend to be in alignment with my core truths, and those things rarely have anything to do with work. My answers are usually about writing, surfing, hiking, reaching out to someone I love, or creating space for lovemaking with my partner. These core needs go way beyond what I could get from working harder, playing more, or earning more money. They're what I must attend to in order to remain in integrity with who I am. If I don't, I get disconnected from my own heart in ways that gnaw at me and require my urgent attention. However, when I'm aligned, I feel free every night, which brings me peace and excellent rest.

DANCING WITH THE FEMININE

PLEASE REMEMBER THAT the principles outlined in this section apply not just to the Feminine in others, but in you as well. As you read, I invite you to reflect on your own wounded, healthy, and sacred Feminine. If you identify as masculine, this effort will also support your understanding of your feminine partner's needs and desires.

The Myth of Not Enough Love

The primary Feminine pain point is almost always about love—or rather the belief that there isn't enough of it. This is true for the Feminine in all of us. I see this expressed in Facebook posts, on various blogs, and endless online articles. I hear it in couples coaching sessions and in the groups I lead. "How can I get him to see me more, cherish me more, show me his feelings more, fuck me longer and with more ferocity or tenderness? How can I get him to support me more in my life, be bolder in his decision making, take charge of the finances, take some of the planning off my plate, or just show up with more presence once in a while?" These are all understandable desires for anyone, but particularly for those with strong feminine essences. They reflect the profound longing to be seen, cherished, and led more fully into the flow of love.

They also reveal the great myth behind much unhappiness and discontent for many feminine-identified beings today—a myth that goes something like, "I'll have enough love when _____," that blank being filled with the right partner, the right kind of sex, the right kind of loving response, and so on. It's a mirage as chronic and pernicious as the masculine myth of not enough freedom, and yet there is nothing wrong with either of them. The problem arises when we vilify others for feeling and acting upon myths that are largely not of their making. As the masculine partner, your charge is to work with this myth compassionately and artfully. This feminine yearning at its core is a natural and beautiful desire for more love—her innate longing to be seen, met, and opened with conscious love.

In its unhealthy form, of course, this desire for more love doesn't usually take the form of the healing and informative gift that it could be. The unhealthy Feminine in all of us is almost always the result of an unmet childhood need that becomes pathological over time. While the origin is never our fault, the habits and responses that occur from it are, in the end, our responsibility. Whether it takes the form of habitual complaint, anxiety, neediness, or reactivity, the manifestation points to a powerful need that only wishes to be seen, healed, and integrated. As the masculine partner, this is where you can come in and meet her—all of her—with empathy, compassion, humor, and love.

The Healthy Feminine—Sharing Your Heart

Many women have developed a healthy means of communicating and sharing their pain of not receiving enough love. The healthy Feminine will share her needs, desires, and pains clearly and honestly with her lover, often in the form of open requests. She can openly share what she needs sexually with her lovers and set healthy boundaries. She maintains a high value on her own self-care and may make more money than her partner without issue. She works hard to develop her own healthy Masculine and become more self-aware. She may take on a spiritual practice that reinforces her capacity for stillness or depth, and she practices conscious communication so that she can clearly express and articulate her desires. She engages in the work it takes to understand her personal neuroses and shadows. She faces her addictions and habits of control. In essence, she does the work to become a healthy and whole human being—capable of understanding, leading, and taking care of herself just fine. This is a beautiful and healthy way of being.

That being said, if she is a truly feminine being, she may still feel lonely, unmet, and frustrated. Despite a seemingly high degree of personal growth, financial success, relational fulfillment, and overall satisfaction, she can still experience a persistent ache in the center of her chest. No matter what she has achieved, she still yearns for something more. The transformational love she craves still eludes her. What has happened, unbeknownst to her, is that her very independence and tendency for self-reliance have also shrouded her heart's wild tenderness. Some part of her is still unrealized and unexpressed. Most feminine beings don't recognize this crisis until it becomes chronic, and they very well may judge their own yearning as unattractive or needy (when, in fact, the opposite is true). Again, the same can be said for your internal Feminine. Sadly, at this point they may start to believe that this ache for more love will never be filled completely. They will either get more resentful and blame the Masculine or seek a deeper surrender to love. Hopefully, they intuit that only a new paradigm will actually evoke the truly sacred intimacy they have been seeking.

The Sacred Feminine—The Gifts of Yearning, Pleasure, and Revealing

In all of us, the sacred Feminine reveals the ache of not being fully seen or felt, the heartbreak at not feeling the flow of love for long enough, and rage at the lack of awareness or numbness in our partner. And the core emotion is the same in all of these expressions—yearning.

This yearning is the chronic, ever-present ache that is the essence of feminine longing. It may be brutal, painful, messy, vulnerable, and terrifying. However, if it can be expressed skillfully, one's partner will find it magnetic. Desire in the feminine body and yearning in the feminine heart is the answer, as opposed to a problem that needs to be solved.

> This sacred Feminine is the embodiment of divine love
> in all spectra of dark and light—Shakti, Kali, Lakshmi,
> Tara, the Morrigan, Freya, Artemis, and Inanna all in one.
> And, at the same time, the Feminine is utterly human.

The sacred Feminine in all of us is concerned with learning how to cultivate the expression of love through our body and present it to the trusted Masculine as an offering of sublime and blissful desire. The Feminine will develop the ability to reveal this tenderness of the heart in a hundred different forms, first and foremost for oneself and for what is personally conceived as the divine. These expressions may take the form of heartfelt rage at a partner's lack of consciousness, as sweet devotion for their mission on the planet, as a divinity who sets the tone of love in the household, as the sacred seductor who surrenders the most taboo sexual desires, as the sorcerer who reveals the subtle energetics most men cannot fathom on their own. The Feminine's body is the instrument for this sacred charge. The Feminine's intention is to evoke the greatest possible consciousness, depth, and leadership from the masculine presence in their life, while always remaining rooted in the truth of their heart. I love the way Kendra Cunov describes this as a new paradigm of feminism that celebrates and empowers *the Feminine*, and not simply women's achievements and parity with men.

The enlightened and sacred Feminine in her will practice seeing through the surface of her partner to the depth of consciousness that is his core essence. She will let that place in him nourish her soul. She is committed to becoming an artist of love who can bring an enormous palette of energies and skills to continually remind him of this essential truth—that he is consciousness. Think of the sacred Feminine as a *dakini* of consciousness—a sky dancer, the enlightened Feminine—above everything else. The Feminine knows their desires and possesses the skill set to communicate them, including the body-mind artistry to evoke the best their partner is capable of in any moment of intimacy. The Feminine has learned to conduct massive amounts of energy through their body, having trained their nervous system to reveal the endless flow of yearning at their core. This sacred Feminine is the embodiment of divine love in all spectra of dark and light—Shakti, Kali, Lakshmi, Tara, the Morrigan, Freya, Artemis, and Inanna all in one. And at the same time, the Feminine is utterly human.

Your role as the masculine partner is to acknowledge, praise, and worship this part of your partner, especially when it is buried beneath the pain and wreckage of modern life. See your partner's divine expression, even when they can't. Use these practices to evoke it, and celebrate the moments they allow you to catch a glimpse of it. Bring your awareness to this place in them as fully as possible, especially during the mundane realities of day-to-day life. Amplify it. Your partner will treasure you for it—just as you treasure them for seeing and loving your nobility, depth, and fierce love.

PRACTICE EXPLORING YOUR OWN FEMININE

Think about your own Feminine in relation to the aspects covered above. Where do you unconsciously look for approval, or recognition? Where do you fall under the spell of the myth that tells you there will be enough love *when* . . . Take an honest look at how you long for your own beauty or emotionality to be seen. Do you expect your emotions to be prioritized above all else in the moment? Is your desire for recognition and safety trying to fill a hole of self-worth inside you, or are you sincerely offering your own radiance and heart as a gift? Next, consider your capacity to feel and express you own natural desires, fears, and longings. Can you communicate them in a healthy manner? Do you judge yourself for your needs or desires? Finally, how in touch and comfortable are you with your own sacred Feminine? Do you reject anything like your own heart's yearning or your body's ability to feel and move pleasure? Or do you offer it to your partner and others as your own natural gift? Ponder all of these questions as clearly and compassionately as you can; your answers will help later on when I suggest ways to shepherd your own Feminine healthfully and artfully.

Step Consciously into Love

Choosing to step into the role of an integrated and sacred masculine partner is no small matter. If you do it with integrity and depth, it will be the most challenging and rewarding practice of your life. When you choose to take responsibility for the heart of your feminine partner in love and consciousness, you must also have the wisdom, clarity, and emotional maturity to understand what comes with the endeavor. Only then can you choose to unabashedly love every single inch of her—with deep awareness and commitment.

She is a whole and complete human, with her own complex relational history. Are there wounds and traumas from her childhood or later in life that inhibit her ability to love fully? Is there residual anger at her father or past lovers who may have been unconscious, clumsy, or downright abusive in their relating? Is she addicted to food, exercise, drugs, drama, or overwork? Did she have a controlling mother who ran the house while her dad passively followed? All of these explorations into her psyche and heart are crucial for you to determine whether she will be someone with whom you want to craft the deepest art. And you should reveal to her and encourage her to artfully inspect your relational and emotional land mines. Two questions are crucial for both of you here: Are you willing to recognize, meet, and support each other's core needs getting met? And then, are you actually capable of that endeavor long term?

Many will simply ignore these questions in favor of the chemicals that result from a steamy sexual connection or the safety and comfort of a potential partnership. Because of the commitment you are making to take each other someplace you could likely not go yourselves, it is crucial to get clear on what exactly you are stepping into. Only then can you lead the relationship with the kind of integrity and depth both of you likely crave. It won't take long. Only a few months of really paying attention are all that's needed, especially to any of each other's blind spots, habitual closures, and land mines. We all have these. What is important is that as the masculine partner in the relationship, you are creating space and attention for artfully examining them before the comfort of long-term relationship creeps in.

Later on in relationships, I see men who will often say they treasure the emotional and sexual connection with their partner—or maybe it's her success in the world—but that her anger is just too much. They might value her sweetness and devotion but cringe at how insecure she can be. Look, if you're honest with yourself, you knew those things about her before making the commitment. You knew about the fury lurking just below the surface; you knew how her parents squashed her self-expression when she was young; you knew about how you triggered each other's abandonment issues. Complaining about these things later on is simply dishonest and unfair.

Instead, you could step into the relationship from the place of wanting to be a source of profound healing and support for her greatest realization as a human being. And you could be clear she wants to do that for you as well. Make the commitment to guide, love, support, challenge, caress, lick, make love to, and completely accept the complexity of who she is—only then will she fully trust you to love her utterly. Not only do you see the depth and beauty of her heart but you also know and choose to be by her side as her greatest ally in the battle for conscious loving.

You are here to help free her heart as the embodiment of presence and depth in her life. You are here to blast the world with devotion, passion, and art together. You are here to support her ability to share love with the world in the way she was born to. There is no greater commitment between two souls, save for becoming a parent. It will test your patience, depth, and relationship to truth, as well as your personal practice and ability to stay present and open in your body.

To truly love the Feminine is to consciously choose all of her, and from there, do your best to co-create with ferocious and impeccable abandon for as long as you can. This is how, one relationship at a time, we can heal the chasm of pain between us—men, women, everyone. And if you can muster the courage and nervous-system strength to take this sacred challenge on, you both will be changed forever. Set aside time to reflect on your feminine partner as she is, and endeavor to get clear on whether you are half-assing it or truly choosing all of her.

PRACTICE ARE YOU WILLING?

In your journal, make a list of your feminine partner's areas of emotional reactivity—anger, jealousy, addiction, fear, shallowness . . . whatever they may be. If you are newly in a relationship with her, get clear on whether you are willing to help her heal in these areas. If you are already committed to her, ask yourself if you are simply ignoring certain areas of closure and shallow relating while hoping they go away. Or are you all in? Either way, gain clarity for yourself and the relationship on whether you are actually choosing all of her. If you truly can't stomach certain aspects, now is the time to ask yourself just how committed to her openness and healing you are. Take your time and be as honest as possible. If the answer is that you truly don't want to support, lead, and love her through these challenges, you should let her know. Then you can choose, later on, whether to take on another relationship after contemplating the same questions.

Your Lack of Conscious Leadership Is a Thousand Pinpricks

Perhaps you and your partner have drifted into a state of numb disconnection. Maybe you are both exhausted from juggling a full workload and home lives with children, or you're so focused on creating success that you've taken your partner's loving and natural gifts for granted. Maybe you haven't kept up with what it takes to do the things that turn each other on and you're less attracted to each other, making sex virtually nonexistent.

For many of us, the stresses of modern life will leach our energy, sex drive, and desire to connect. The focus and energy needed to create whatever you call your empire are pretty much all a person can manage, so it should be no surprise when disconnection and disagreements follow. Her complaints about how present you once were or how much time you used to enjoy together may become amplified and more contentious. Perhaps you start to feel unappreciated or constantly challenged about how you spend your time and energy. You might notice your partner working more or taking more time for her own personal development, or note that she's filling her schedule with other endeavors—your kids or her friends, for example.

You might still occasionally connect while all of the above is going on—usually after a fight (and with promises to do better or more for each other)—but the momentum is clear: your default is increased disconnection. The tide's too strong to swim against, so the relationship ends. You felt you just couldn't win, so you gave up. Maybe somebody new will appreciate you more fully.

Or maybe you're the good guy. Maybe you're caring and kind. You have reverence for the Feminine, you have lots of love to give, and you yearn for someone to share your life with. Even so, partners won't fully share their hearts. You might go on lots of dates and enjoy lots of meaningful short relationships, but the Feminine seem hesitant or tepid to dive in with you. You do what you can to encourage something more long-term and lasting—you offer them even more care and attention, you listen attentively, you make them elaborate dinners—but it's always the same story. Eventually they become more distant and non-responsive; sometimes they ghost you completely.

Something is wrong with both of these pictures. What is it?

The answer is actually simple, so simple that most men miss it: *You haven't led her into a deeper experience of her own heart.*

As the unconscious masculine partner above, you have been too self-centered to feel how much pain she is in, mistaking her feedback as mere nagging and complaining. As the good guy featured above, you assumed she wanted sweetness and gentleness, when what she really craved was confidence, strong presence, and to feel the leader in you.

In both cases, what's missing is getting in touch with what her heart most desires and then leading her there with strength, presence, and awareness. Any human with a feminine essence wants to be playfully and passionately guided into the deepest realms of sexual and emotional intimacy. Many a would-be masculine partner has ignored this critical aspect of leadership, and the result is confusion, resentment, and disconnection. Ultimately, a partner in their Feminine wants to experience the full-body remembrance that, at their core, *is* love. They don't want to continually have to explain this to you.

Your feminine partner wants *you* to feel what the relationship, the date, or the sex needs at any moment and then artfully and sensitively guide from that knowing. Every step of the way, feeling and checking in with her. And so, every time she is taken in the opposite direction, every time her feminine nature is unseen or ignored, every time she is called upon to lead herself in intimacy because you are simply too distracted, unconscious, or self-centered, it pains her in ways the Masculine will never comprehend.

When there is a lack of integral, trustable, and playful masculine leadership in her love life, a person with a strong feminine essence will feel starved and resentful. They often won't even know why. The things you do will irritate them more. The seemingly innocuous habits you've had for years will become sources of snarky comments, judgments, and disconnection. They may become less attracted to you and fill more of their time with tasks and duties rather than be attuned to the flow of love and devotion in their body. They may start to become attracted to others who display the traits of boldness and confidence they crave, and they may even seek out partners who display those characteristics. It's as true on your first date as it is on your twenty-first anniversary.

Take responsibility for the relationship;
take responsibility from the core.

Most masculine-identified men, when faced with the above—an annoyed, distracted, or wandering lover—have no idea what's happening. All they see is something they want to stop, change, or magically improve, all the while ignoring the basic fact that they are responsible for looking the other way as they allowed this dynamic to take hold. If either of these scenarios is happening in your life, *you* had a big hand in it.

Each unconscious abdication of leadership in the relationship is a pinprick to her heart. Over the course of years, thousands of these moments will scar or harden her. She didn't enter into the relationship complaining and unhappy; she entered with a sincere desire to finally reveal and share the most sacred part of her to someone she could completely trust. As time went by and she felt your lack of presence, awareness, and attention, she grew increasingly angry. Before that, she probably felt sad, but quickly after that came the anger. That's probably when she tried to do what she could to fix the problem—relationship counseling, books on communication styles, more personal development, and so on. But it was never her problem to fix in the first place.

The simple solution here is to become conscious as to where the problem has taken hold and make an unshakable decision. Take responsibility for the relationship; take responsibility from the core. It's actually not as difficult as it sounds. But it does take a cultivation of awareness and feeling, as well as strength of conviction. The following is a simple exercise to help you get started in your exploration. I encourage you to set aside time for this reflection and to commit to ruthless honesty. It will only serve you—and her.

PRACTICE **MAKE A RELATIONAL INVENTORY**

Feel into your relationship right now and make an honest assessment of what you find in a journal. What isn't working? Where are her needs or yours not being met? What important truths are you withholding? What skills do you both need to learn to take the relationship to a higher place? Get clear on these points and then apologize for letting things slide for as long as you have. Address it squarely and make a plan to take the relationship to the next level. If your partner is truly feminine in their essence, something profound will relax in them. I have seen many women (and men) even weep. The experience of being led well in love this way—that is, from the part of you committed to integrity, depth, and growth—will profoundly change their life and your relationship, as well.

Know the Difference Between (Unconsciously) Making Her Lead and (Consciously) Sharing Leadership

Over the past century, we have gone from the masculine paradigm of authoritarianism to a nascent approach of equitable co-creation. It's easy for us to forget that women have only had the right to vote in most Western countries for a hundred years, at most. The world has changed rapidly, and something wonderful and new is coming into being. But at the same time, many men are uncertain how to conduct themselves and live in a new paradigm marked with embodied, consciousness-driven, love-centered leadership.

Much of this book is dedicated to this issue. When am I supposed to lead? What's that even mean? When do I just let it flow, and when is it her turn? How do I move back and forth between her leadership and my own? And how can we do all of this consciously while staying connected to the meta flow of love with the intention of serving each other and the world?

I want to be clear that nobody is supposed to own the Masculine pole and lead impeccably 24/7. That would be impossible, not to mention exhausting. You do, however, need to cultivate the awareness and communication needed to help her flow between her Masculine and Feminine as they arise. This is simply setting you both up to win. That being said, the bigger problem doesn't involve sharing in this way, but in unconsciously expecting her to take the lead.

If there is an area in your life in which you are less than integral, or there is chronic disconnection in your relationship, she will be *compelled* to address it. Meanwhile, you're probably more invested in whether you are winning in your chosen game of life; or how to best manage your time, money, and energy; or whether you have enough freedom to enjoy your life. The Masculine in all of us is compelled to focus on these things.

But assuming that she is more feminine in her essence, she will feel the pain of your disconnection and incongruence more acutely, and she will invariably step into the vacuum of your poor leadership. She will not be able to help herself. One of the more detrimental by-products of our current age is that women are encouraged to apply the skill set they have developed in their professional lives to address their broken hearts, and it doesn't work. In fact, it tends to foster more disconnection and heartache.

We as men have sat back and watched too long without really understanding our complicity in the suffering of women in romantic relationships. One handy example of this is in the bedroom. If she feels your numbness, boredom, or lack of presence in bed, it will truly pain her. You might be supplementing your sexuality with porn (she might be, too), thinking that it will ease the pain. Meanwhile, she will intuit that there is more possible than what you're experiencing together, and she'll want to step in to create more—checking out podcasts on the topic, for example, or suggesting posts and articles to read. She may sign you both up for a sexual intimacy workshop or just complain repetitively in order to shake you from your lethargy. What she's doing is trying to solve the problem, because you aren't.

*If she's better suited to take charge, make
the request and get out of her way.*

Unfortunately, her efforts will tend to have the opposite effect on your attraction to her, which in turn will only amplify the pain. In response, she might try harder (becoming more aggressive in bed), voice her concerns louder, or even seek out an affair. All of this is her attempt at fixing what you didn't prioritize.

Her actions aren't preferable—especially not to her. They are merely the by-product of your unwillingness to step in and take 100 percent responsibility for the toxic dynamic you have ignored or allowed to take root. But the moment you stand up and take ownership and present a plan that feels good to her, I guarantee you that things will change. Acknowledge her pain and the problem, and she'll relax. Why? Because the Feminine is always wanting more of your embodied conscious awareness.

It's also just as appropriate to ask her to lead. She could very well be more capable of doing so. However, if that's the case, you can still acknowledge the situation, apologize for your part in creating it, recognize her leadership qualities, and make a direct request for her to take charge of the situation. This type of open-hearted acknowledgement of the issue— without blame—is, in its own right, a form of leadership, and one that promotes mutual love and freedom. So, if she's better suited to take charge, make the request and get out of her way. It won't do for you to drag ass or complain about her choices. Even if she's taking the lead, she'll still need to feel your commitment and the depth of your love for her.

The same is true for times when you are emotionally bereft and need to be heard, seen, and listened to. This is your beautiful Feminine on display, and it is an integral part of who you are as a man. However, you must be conscious of when your Feminine needs to be attended to. If you come home from work feeling afraid or defeated and ask if you can just fall apart and complain about life for a few minutes, she will more than likely be happy to hold that space for you. But if you charge into the room unconsciously dumping your complaint and pain onto her when she isn't prepared to respond or when she is in her Feminine and is expecting your presence, the situation will likely devolve. If you clearly establish the container for your own Feminine to be held by her Masculine, you are leading even as you are falling apart, and she will love you for it. This has been a revelation for me and many others I teach.

The masculine's primary gift is to feel into what will create the most openness, growth, and love, and from there to lead the relationship to that place. Co-creating your relationship is a beautiful experience, and leadership should always be shared according to who's better at a certain task, what's needed to create the most love and nourishment in the moment, and what's most conducive to the growth of the relationship and each of you as individuals. I can't recommend highly enough the skill of leading while following.

PRACTICE **RELATIONAL LEADERSHIP DIALOGUE**

Begin by setting a container for dialogue—an agreed upon amount of time that will be free of distraction. Sit down together and talk about what each of you is best at in the relationship, even if it doesn't exactly align with either of your preferences. Let her tell you where she would love your leadership to play more of a role. Take turns. Tell her what you want and ask how she feels. Then craft a plan moving forward that consciously takes all of this into consideration. Maybe she's better at the finances, but she really hates doing it. In this example (and, of course, if you're financially in a situation to do so), look into hiring a bookkeeper. It might take more money than you want to spend, but the value you'll get in return from her knowing that you're prioritizing the relationship and her happiness will be more than worth it. Take charge of the areas you're better at, and let her do what she's more inclined to do. Show her that you're aware of *who* should be leading and *when*. It will do wonders for your dynamic.

She Wants to Go Someplace She Can't Lead Herself

Men often ask me why a certain woman isn't interested in them. Why didn't she say yes to a second date? Why did she go cold—seemingly out of nowhere—after six months? Why is my feminine partner uninterested in me sexually? The length and form of the relationship is less important than the actual texture of the problem. Her heart is closed to you; she doesn't feel lit up when she's around you. So, what happened?

It seemed like there were more than a few moments where she was interested, maybe even excited!

A primary reason that a feminine partner leaves a relationship (or cuts off a possible relationship) is because she doesn't trust you to lead her into the place of her heart she has been longing to go. This is the place she can't lead herself. It is a place of surrender, trust, opening, and sacred submission. It is a place where she can completely let you see all of her—whether it be a ruthless warrior, driven mogul, or devotional dark lover. It is a place she may even be afraid of. Her pain lives there, as well as her insecurities. The only reason a healthy, independent, prospective feminine partner is interested in you at all is because she is hoping you can help her experience transformational love with the utmost integrity and depth.

That's why she went on a date with you. Maybe on the surface it was about partnership or sex or just having a good time, but underneath it she wanted to experience the divine bliss of being seen and felt completely from the place of your conscious awareness and capacity to feel. Poets, songwriters, and countless authors have written about it for centuries. Cultures around the world have created rituals to honor the beautiful (as well as fierce and devotional) way the integrated Masculine and Feminine are magnetically drawn together. Children in the East were trained from early ages to become practitioners in the play of yin and yang, Shiva and Shakti. This archetypal passion lives in the heart of every human.

Religion and the rigors of modern living may have twisted and dampened it over the centuries, but it still burns in the core of our hearts. The yearning for sacred union is a unique aspect of who we are; it will never be extinguished. It only takes a certain glance or touch or moment for the spark to become ignited and we remember: *this is why we are alive.* And the more identified with this desire we are, the more we are in our Feminine—regardless of our gender.

So, when a feminine partner loses interest in you, it is not a question of the details. It's simply because she lost trust in your ability to take her to this ancient and sacred place.

Somewhere along the line, you may have lost your nerve with her and been obsequious or obliging. You may have kept the conversation light and polite or safely on the surface. Perhaps you spent most of the time talking about your career, bank account, or other things you mistakenly thought might impress her. You may have been uninterested in connecting more profoundly with her due to your own obligations or life pressures. You may have settled for ten-minute sex when she was hoping you'd ravish her for hours. There are a million different reasons a woman decides you are not the "one," but the primary issue is the same. She intuits something greater that she knows is possible, and she has decided that you aren't the one to take her there.

Years ago, when I was out on a date with an extremely beautiful and successful woman, I remembered telling myself, *She's definitely out of your league, John.* But I did my best to practice what I had been learning and teaching—I remained present, I breathed into my belly, and I placed my awareness squarely on her heart and body. There was a moment about halfway through our lunch that I could feel the experience sliding off into mediocrity and disconnection. I can't remember what it was . . . something akin to her talking abstractly about her career or her family or her ex-partner. Whatever it was, I knew where the conversation was taking us, and I knew it wasn't what she wanted from me.

So, I looked her in the eyes and gently but firmly said, "Stop talking." Then I took a long pause and said, "I want to feel you." I looked into her eyes and began to feel into the core of her heart. I don't know how long we looked at each other—maybe thirty seconds, maybe longer—but eventually something opened between us and she revealed herself, even tearing up in the moment she felt me see her so deeply. I smiled and said, "There she is," and we both laughed. The rest of the date was energized, erotic and intensely connected.

Neither of us wanted to go through the same expected prattle. And what she really wanted was to be seen and have me experience the love and devotion at her core. She wanted to have a greater experience of being guided there in a way that felt good in her body; she just didn't know how to get there by herself. Of course, she could have found a way without any help from me, but when I recognized the shallow direction of our connection and presented a whole new possibility she wasn't fully aware of, my value as a potential romantic and sexual partner grew tremendously. More than that, we each grew past our habits, and more love was created and liberated in that moment.

She Yearns to Experience You as Embodied Consciousness

A man who has a profound connection to the Infinite is a grounding force, and the Feminine will view him as an emotional and sexual gift. The constantly shifting Feminine in all of us is comforted and relaxed by the masculine relationship to that which never changes. The reverse is also true. If a man has little awareness of the infinite nature of life, his presence will more often than not create tension in the feminine nervous system, and she will always feel slightly malnourished and long for someone who can ground her.

The more identified with the Feminine a person is, the more they are subject to the shifting weather patterns of mood and feeling. This is true in all of us. One moment it's sunny and breezy, the next is cold and sullen. The beauty of the Feminine in life and in each of us is that it reflects the profoundly and often suddenly changing nature of life itself. From the gentle meadow to the raging volcano, the Feminine can be a terrifying and destructive force or a nourishing, gentle, and life-giving spring. And like tropical weather, it can change in an instant.

Suppose you're with a feminine partner who is (as they say) *a force of nature*. She has a power that runs through her body that practically anyone present can feel. She is both alive and alluring, but also dangerous in her capacity to run energy. We all know someone like this, and your Masculine is often magnetically drawn to women like this. They are typically beloved and sought after as entertainers, entrepreneurs, and leaders. All of us carry this energetic signature to some degree, although few know how to harness and utilize it artfully. The more this force of nature is present, the more they will be drawn to a masculine that can express consciousness through his body. The Masculine partner who can apply stillness, breath, and presence to a relational moment will provide safety and structure to her energy, and she can relax emotionally and sexually. It's an incredible experience for a highly energetic feminine being to feel this through their body.

A man fully vested in his purpose is inherently
attractive and more trustable.

In electricity, the stronger the current, the more dangerous and unpredictable it can be, and the more it needs to be tethered to a stable, grounded, unchanging source. This is what a masculine partner can provide vis-à-vis the structure of his physical presence, breath, and posture, in addition to his connection to the core of himself and of life.

PRACTICE SENSING AND CONNECTING

The next time you are near a feminine being you're involved with romantically, begin to breathe into your lower abdomen. Feel your lower body—legs, genitals, and feet. Breathe into your belly, cultivating an awareness and heaviness in your legs, and relax the front surface of your body. Relax your mind as if unclenching a fist. Feel into the part of you that is unchanging and infinite. From this state, make an intention to not just feel consciousness but *be* consciousness. Do your best to match your breath to hers. When she inhales, you inhale. When she exhales, you exhale. Even if you can't catch her breath, imagine you are breathing for her. Begin to feel inside her body and nervous system as if you could discern the sensations and tensions therein. Feel for any tightness in her belly, heart, throat, or jaw, and relax that area in yourself while continuing to feel her. Notice what happens to her. Does she slow down? Turn to you? Release the tension in her shoulders? Chances are—if you hold this pose long enough—you will evoke from her a relaxed openness. This is the practice of actively grounding, relaxing, and opening a lover—even if you are just sitting next to each other at dinner. You can even begin to time how long it takes to get an obvious opening or hint of relaxation from her. It won't take long. And you will have learned how to use your body as a conductor of consciousness that can evoke openness in your lover but also a group of strangers, your children, or even a given space.

She Desires a Man Who Lives with Purpose

A man tethered to consciousness will inevitably begin to feel that life itself is trying to push through him into the world. The more aligned with the Infinite he is (and not simply his own monkey mind), the more the cosmos will speak to him to create. It is his job to listen but also to align everything in his world to this transmission, as Deida pointed out in *The Way of the Superior Man*. Any masculine-identified person fully vested in their purpose is inherently attractive and more trustable, whereas someone who is disconnected or unconscious comes across as a bit lost. He may meet with worldly success, but the Feminine will mistrust him and view him as lacking purpose and direction.

A radiant and powerful feminine partner wants to know you can feel and express consciousness through your body; she also wants to see you press that consciousness into the world as a powerful mission. She will be disappointed if you don't display your depth fully to the world, if you instead choose to prioritize material comfort, or if your life is not aligned with the gift you are meant to give to the world. These things are exactly what her heart and body will equate as impotence. She will not trust you to lead her into the most sublime spaces of her own heart if you can't make real your own creative yearnings.

Now, this is not to say you have to know your core mission at all times. But the important thing to remember in those invariable times of forgetfulness or lostness is that you still have something uniquely *you* that wants to be expressed. Perhaps your deepest consciousness just needs to relax after a long period of output; maybe you need to travel or go on some sort of solo adventure, or finally get in shape, or perhaps spend time in silent retreat. Whatever it is, it's crucial not to employ those periods of uncertainty as further reason to distract yourself or waste energy on shallow pursuits.

> Simply put, most men don't know how to home
> in on and work with the truth of their pain.

Your particular life's mission needn't be grandiose or heroic. Not everyone is supposed to devote themselves to bringing fresh water to remote villages in Sudan. Very often, your life's mission simply comes down to sensing what *the next right thing* is and stepping into it with boldness and commitment. It could be as simple as deepening your connection to the divine or getting in the best shape of your life. Someone with a feminine essence will want to know you are self-aware enough to navigate these twists and turns with clarity and strong intention. If you do so, she will relax and trust your leadership, because it will be clear to her and others that you are capable of skillfully leading yourself.

She Needs a Man Who Can Handle Himself — and Her

For almost fifty years now, men have been taught that it is crucial to get in touch with their feelings and learn how to express them. Men in particular have gone to great lengths to buck toxic and stoic masculine archetypes and have rebelled against working themselves to death and stuffing feelings of grief, loneliness, and self-doubt. In countless ways, men of the past several decades have developed a new relationship with their own radiance, with the flow of life, and their own emotional bodies. All of this was much needed, and it's an integral step to developing healthier relationships.

Unfortunately, they haven't always been taught the commensurate means to develop their own healthy and spiritual Masculine in ways that will also promote and treasure their Feminine. They have not been taught how to use the spiritual principles of awareness, breath, and relaxation to *be with* the intense emotions of modern living. They have not developed skills of emotional awareness that allow them to identify the sources of their discomfort and pain, let alone communicate them. Simply put, most men don't know how to home in on and work with the truth of their pain.

This means that we have several generations who can feel deeply without knowing what to do about it. Far too often, they judge their own yearnings and feelings of neediness as problematic or weak. And rather than find healthy outlets for their intensity, they too often fall into rage, jealousy, numbness, grief, shame, and loneliness. They may spiritually bypass their darker feelings in favor of positive affirmations or — in contrast — indulge their own emotionality to the point of narcissism. This latter critique is far too often applicable to what passes for "men's work."

When a primarily masculine partner overindulges in their own emotions without creating structure to hold it, they will invariably compete with the emotionality of the feminine partner. A power struggle will then ensue — shouting matches, finger pointing, the works — because there is no clear understanding or agreement between partners of who is expressing emotion (the Feminine) and who is the witness (the Masculine).

Clearly, the skill set men have been given to deal with their emotions is lacking. And the way this often comes across to a feminine partner is that you can't even hold your own difficult or dark emotions, so how in the world can you hold hers? And so, when someone with a truly feminine essence cries out in frustration, "Just handle me!," as I have seen in myriad ways, they are straightforwardly expressing the desire to be held, seen, and led through a bout of emotional turmoil from a place of calm depth.

They're pleading for you to keep your ground and not get swayed by their storms. They don't want you to kowtow when they are mean or disconnected from their hearts; they want you to either playfully move them out of it or set a boundary they can respect. They want you to behold their grief or rage—to witness it with clarity and acceptance—and to see it as a beautiful part of who they are. They don't want you to put up with their shit. Just as they shouldn't put up with yours. They want you to show up and prove you aren't easily triggered by their shifting moods. They want you to use your strength and depth to alchemize whatever's arising into love.

A masculine partner who can truly respond to feminine emotionality with playful skill, clarity, feeling, and grounded presence is remarkably valuable. And it goes without saying that men wanting to cultivate this capacity must start with themselves. She's right: if you can't handle your own storms, moods, fears, and grief, how in the world can you handle hers?

MAKE SEX AN ART

Become an Artist of Love

Hearing this concept from David Deida, that sex is an art, was revolutionary for me. I have come to understand the profundity that every moment together can be artful and that our bodies are the paint and the canvas. This reframe completely changed the trajectory of my romantic life. As in any artistic practice—whether it be playing a musical instrument, teaching a college course, or developing a piece of software—your subtlety and skill will require hours of practice and refinement. True masters of anything spend thousands of hours learning and honing their craft; the art of your sexuality is no different.

Every day, you have an opportunity to refine how you bring presence, consciousness, and love to your romantic partner. It might be as subtle as how you make them a morning cup of coffee or as obvious as how you please them with oral sex. You are either purposefully refining the way you transmit, share, and penetrate your partner with love, or you are unconsciously playing out your karmic impulses to get off and have comfort. There's really not a lot of in-between.

It all begins with setting an intention. What do you wish to create in your lovemaking? How do you want to create it? The details will almost always become clear when your intention is strong and your body full of energy and breath. But without a strong intention—to worship her body, to defile her sacredly, to make her feel like the most beautiful creature on the planet, or to heal her soul—you will likely remain in the realm of simple pleasure seeking.

There's nothing wrong with pleasure. Amplifying the pleasure and energy in a polarized sexual moment is a crucial role of whoever is playing the feminine partner. And whoever is playing the masculine will be charged with bringing that pleasure and physical connection to a deeper space. Sublime art requires energy, but also truth. Think of the most moving music, the most intricate paintings, the complex dramas and insights of literature . . . all of these share a combination of energy and the penetrating truths of human experience. In the same way, making sex an art requires bringing your masculine gifts of clarity, structure, penetration, and awareness to each romantic moment, while simultaneously allowing for the flow of pleasure—both hers and yours.

Sex Is the Deepest Yoga

We all carry the residue of our relational and sexual past. Over the years, we collect various wounds and scars, and they collect in the center column of our bodies—that tube of nerves and energetic meridians between our throat and genitals. Every time we felt the wavering of our parents' love, every time we received early shame messages about our sexual desires, every time we were rejected by a coveted lover—all of these experiences added kinks to the center of our nervous systems, and these kinks became paired with one of the quite common thought-forms meant to protect ourselves from the hurt: *I'm bad. It's never enough. No one will ever love me.*

These and similar sentiments become well-defended stories in our body-minds. As time goes on, we begin to take the subtle shapes of these habitual beliefs, closures, and tightenings. Your chest might start to cave protectively, your face may turn sour, the front of your body may develop a shield to armor you from possible rejection or abuse. If you pay attention, you can observe others manifest these subtle closures or recognize them in your own body.

After years of contorting our bodies like this, our thinking becomes solidified around sex and relationships. We develop stories that match the stored wounds, and this is how the relationship karma of our lives takes hold. You may have vowed as a younger man to never become your father (or mother), and yet when you attempt to open your heart and sex to those who want to love you, there they are in the tightness and patterns that arise beyond your control. The scars of your unrequited love and unexpressed desires impede your capacity to conduct love through your body.

If we are to unwind the accumulation of personal history and trauma in our bodies (generational and cultural) and begin to relate from the core, we need to commit ourselves to opening. It must come from the inside out of our psychosexual and emotional bodies, and the endeavor is not something that can be willed by the mind. The tentacles of these wounds run too deep.

What I have found practicing and teaching this concept is that clearing calls for traumas stored in our genitals, sacrum, and the floor of our pelvis to be released and moved out of our bodies. We need to free up the space needed for love and consciousness to move in. This is the work of sexual yoga.

The breathwork and embodiment practices that I learned from my teachers have been passed down from ancient traditions and can open long-clogged energetic channels in your body and nervous system. Yogic sexuality entails running breath, awareness, and energy through these stuck areas while cultivating a profound openness. As in traditional yoga, many of the asanas (or postures) are ongoing. For example, the Downward Dog pose is standard in basic yoga. In this foundational asana, the practitioner presses their thumbs and forefingers into the ground while raising their seat toward the ceiling, wrapping triceps inward, bringing their chest toward their thighs, and driving their heels gently toward the floor. The intention is one of physical openness, to which there is no end.

> It won't take long for the grip of trauma to loosen
> up and transmute into love and sexual energy.

In a similar fashion, the asanas of sexual yoga require simultaneous attention to multiple gestures of openness. For example, the masculine partner must cultivate a strong spine, fully embodied breath, relaxed frontal body, and penetrative yet loving eye contact with a partner. He must also ground into the earth, raise his heart, widen his awareness, and so on. Often these "gestures" seem in opposition to one another—for example, the sacrum lifting upward as the heels root downward—however, the pose is what occurs in the balancing between the opposing intentions and *attentions*. And, to restate the point, none of these gestures ever reach completion. They could go on forever, deepening further into the infinite spaces of love and consciousness.

Unlike traditional yoga, sexual yoga practice is relational—whether it be with another human, a group, your environment, or the present moment. You are witnessed by a partner with unconditional regard, staying open and connected no matter what the pose calls for. This is much more challenging than solo practice, but the rewards have an alchemizing effect on the hearts and nervous systems of both practitioners.

The Three-Part Breath practice I described earlier will change and open up your channels and create space for more energy and love to flow. It can even challenge you emotionally, as it has the power to pop the top off stored wounds in your body-mind. Done consistently, these and other practices expand your nervous system capacities immensely, and it won't take long for the grip of trauma to loosen up and transmute into love and sexual energy.

PRACTICE THREE-PART BREATH AND SEX

This is a Taoist breath practice that can be done solo or with a partner. First, create a sacred container (e.g., a dedicated time and space) for sexual connection. Try starting with thirty minutes and expand from there. Sexual practice of any kind has the power to unearth long-held emotion, so it's crucial that you allow enough time to hold the more challenging feelings that may arise. Follow the directions for the Three-Part Breath practice in section 3 and stay present with your sensations and emotions as you pleasure yourself sexually. If engaging this practice with a partner, invite them to witness you by looking into your eyes, praising you with their words, or even just consciously breathing and feeling you. She can even share her own pleasure and yearning, your combined practice becoming an offering to the divine rather than something that remains hidden in shame and indignity.

Bringing our wounds—especially sexual wounding—into partnered practice allows us to release long-felt shame around sexuality. A once-painful area is now bathed in pleasure and devotion while sexual energy is flowing through the center channel—clearing any closures. The more sexual energy running through the system, the more the knots untie. New neural pathways get created and link together, and you will become increasingly free to enjoy an entirely new relationship with masturbation.

While this type of practice is far from easy, the effects are nothing short of profound. Deeply stored wounds clear up and transmute into self-love, compassion, and sexual energy. Engaged wholeheartedly, people often discover parts of themselves long buried as the shame lifts. When we allow ourselves to be seen by our partner in these ways, we create uncommon intimacy.

The key is to harness the creative power of sexual energy. When you can guide it through the deepest parts of your body while being witnessed in love, you rewire your nervous system. No traditional yoga or therapeutic path can emulate the profundity of this work, in which all of your fears, shame, and taboos can be healed in ecstatic openness. There are rules of structure, of course (just as in traditional yoga), but within that structure you'll find room for incredible creativity and vulnerability.

Create Sacred Containers for Sex

Imagine a recent event in your personal or work life that was important to you. Maybe you gave a speech or a presentation to a group of respected peers, had an opportunity to land a new client, put together an important business deal, or opened a studio to display your art. Perhaps you wrote a book or published an important article in your field, or maybe you became passionate about a particular hobby—playing piano, tango dancing, tennis, or golf. Whatever the case may be, bring to mind this achievement and reflect on the level of preparation, intention, perseverance, and presence you brought to that endeavor or new passion.

How much time and money did you invest? How many hours did you spend preparing and fine-tuning? How long did it take you to assess and understand the subtle nuances involved? Odds are you put a tremendous amount of energy and intention into nailing the presentation or mastering your game, down to even the most minute details.

Now, compare that approach and focus to how you show up for sex and your relationship. If you're like most humans, there's a distinct gap. The reasons for this vary, but the common thread is that people typically don't frame their sex life in the same way they would their hobbies or their mission in the world—as a commitment to an *art form*. Given how important sexual intimacy is to our overall happiness, it's heartbreaking that most people don't treat it with the reverence and intentionality it deserves.

We may have been taught to show up for the physical aspects of sex, believing that nature would take care of the rest. We would arrive at each experience already attracted to our partners, our hearts would automatically be open, and sexual energy would just naturally flow. We would know what to do, and we'd have the confidence and skill set to do it. In fact, we've been trained to believe something is likely wrong with us if this doesn't happen naturally. But in long-term partnerships, that's often not the case.

Mind-blowing, soul-healing, life-changing sex begins with an intentional, detailed preparation to create something special for both of you.

And yes, there is an art to it. How you prepare yourself and your lover for sex is as important as the sex itself, if not more so. It is in this meticulous space of creation that your devotion and generosity can melt any resistances, traumas, and habits (your partner's and your own), releasing the strangle that blocks the inherent flow of love. The success of any important endeavor is the by-product of the unwavering intention and preparation behind it, and this is doubly true in love.

What if you treated an entire day leading up to sex as a crucial part of your lovemaking experience? What if you used the time prior to coming together to amplify your devotion, desire, and love for your partner? What if you spent more time looking into her eyes, breathing with her, feeling the contours and nuances of her body? All without the goal of getting off. Just letting love swell. This is how you can prepare your canvas with meticulous reverence and devotion.

Couples will go numb around the intentional and sacred design of their bedrooms and simply have sex among baby toys, dirty clothes, and the other debris of life—content to have a few moments of pleasure and connection amid the monotony of their daily routine. While there is nothing wrong with that, there always exists a richer possibility—a possibility that will amplify the love and pleasure you want to experience together.

What if your bedroom was a temple of your passion for each other, created and appointed in your own personal, heartfelt ways? Can you feel how that might bring more art to your sex? Understanding that the masculine partner's sexual gift is structure and the feminine partner's gift is energy, imagine ways those gifts can manifest in the environment you create for each other. The result will be magic.

PRACTICE **CREATING YOUR CONTAINER**

Creating a space for your sex that is the physical manifestation of your conscious love will soothe and relax your feminine partner. Think about as many details as you possibly can—the time you'll be meeting for sex, whether you'll meet together or one of you will be waiting for the other—as well as your intention (e.g., offering pleasure, receiving pleasure, stress relief, making a baby, or creating a healing, spiritual experience for both of you). Clarity in these areas will foster trust in your feminine partner and depth in your sex, and all of these details come together to create the anatomy of your experience together. Don't scrimp, and don't cut corners. Use candles, music, fabric, props, an altar, or whatever else inspires you. You are taking your partner on a journey. Is there a playlist for that journey? Should there be a mirror involved? Incense? Flowers? Chocolate? Handcuffs? Is this a darker, more primal space? Or is it tender and sweet?

And remember, the container for your sex is not simply the physical space. It entails the energetic and emotional realms as well. If your goal is for your partner to be in their Feminine, make sure they do not have to think about anything. Be meticulous around the time and instructions for them. Lovingly but firmly guide them into a bath; have a glass of wine or a piece of chocolate ready. Show her that you've covered every angle of the experience, including cleaning the space, managing the childcare, or anything else that could distract either of you. Quickies are great, but an artful and deeply intimate relationship requires a steady diet of conscious, intentional, and even shamanic sexual practice. If you make your bedroom a temple of consciousness and love, your sex and love will reflect it.

Many people come to bed at night still clinging to the remnants of the day's tasks and duties, and their heads are filled with the endless details that need attending to. In this atmosphere, sexual intimacy is often an afterthought. Maybe it will happen; maybe not. Most couples rely on the sex itself to bring them into their bodies—unconsciously, of course. Further, most will not allow for extra time to drop into their masculine or feminine essences and will come to bed energetically neutral. Two magnets that have been rubbed together all day will typically repel each other, which tends to make for short and unfulfilling sexual intimacy.

Instead, try to consciously prepare your body for conducting and receiving love from either the Masculine or Feminine pole. It doesn't take long. Ten minutes of attentive polarity practice will create a much more powerful charge before you even touch one another. The following is a simple example, but feel free to improvise as you grow in your practice.

Embrace the Art of Sexual Polarity

Your embodied consciousness is a sexual gift. A masculine partner who has a profound connection to both the Infinite and the earth is a grounding force. The constantly shifting Feminine in all of us is comforted and relaxed by the Masculine relationship to that which is solid and that which never changes. The reverse is also true. If a man has no or little awareness of the infinite nature of life, if he lacks the grounding I've talked about in this book, his presence will create tension in the feminine nervous system, and she will always feel malnourished and long for someone who can settle her more fully in the present moment.

She wants to feel you as the embodiment of masculine sexual polarity, not simply as being present. And as I have mentioned before, there's a substantial difference between simply being present and holding an embodied presence. To restate it, *being present* means you are aware of the moment and much of what it contains (smells, sounds, people, energies). *Having an embodied presence* in sex means that you are pressing the infinite nature of this moment through your body, especially the belly and genitals, into the center of your partner's body. There is more weight to it. More space. More groundedness. In a sexual or relational moment, this texture of embodying the Infinite is incredibly pleasurable to a feminine-identified partner. This is just as true in same-sex or gender-fluid relating. Who is the masculine and feminine here can be a complete matter of choice. Surrendering open to receive consciousness is the essential feminine practice, regardless of gender or sexual orientation.

The more naturally energetic your feminine partner is, the more she will be drawn to a masculine partner who can express the weight and depth of consciousness through his body and who can be still and deep in a moment of chaos. This will ground any part of her that is wild and untethered, while simultaneously giving her permission to express the full range of her heart—even sadness, grief, and rage. Or, if she is typically unexpressed due to trauma or having to hold the Masculine in her own work, your capacity to express presence through your body will draw her feminine essence more to the surface, and she will be able to relax more emotionally and sexually.

As Deida explains, the masculine partner's gift of structure is a state of embodied presence that can effortlessly draw this potential out. To be clear, structure is distinct from control. In sex and relating, the Masculine capacity to ready, hold, and direct the movement of time and space in service of love relaxes the feminine heart and nervous system. Your awareness and precise attention to what would feel best is crucial in helping the Feminine let go of control. She will not need to hold the space or apply her awareness to bring tasks to completion, as she may increasingly have to do in daily life. She can let go and trust you to create a container with your breath, body, and awareness that will allow her to relax into feeling, expression, pleasure, and devotion. All of this occurs in her heart and nervous system as sexual, even if you aren't having sex yet. Consider the following:

- *I started a bath for you. Why don't you get in and then come to bed?*
- *Let's meet together tonight at 9 p.m. after the kids are asleep.*
- *Let's go to Santa Barbara for the weekend.*
- *I have work all week, but let's plan Saturday afternoon to have a date together.*

All of these are structure statements. They allude to where and when love is going to be honored, explored, and celebrated. Anyone in their Feminine needs to know the wheres and whens of the encounter or they will begin to feel anxious: How long are you going to be together? How long apart? When together, what will you be doing? Having sex, eating dinner, taking a hike? When planning time together, the masculine gifts of clarity and structure make themselves known in the answers of these details.

She needs to feel that your capacity to plan and implement details is greater than hers, if only for a short while. If not, she may have to step in and take over creating the structure for your relationship, and that rarely will feel good for her (or you most of the time). The amount of pain I have seen this cause women who want nothing more than to let go of directing is staggering—they can't be both the energy *and* the structure. Not if the goal is sexual polarity, at least.

You should know, however, that until she trusts your ability to create and manage this type of structure, she'll most likely resist it. She may be carrying stress and overwhelm that occurs as a forgetting that more love is possible. And this is where most of us give up. Our cultural programming, fears of rejection, aversion to coming across as too dominant, and our lack of understanding that the core Feminine desires to be led, opened, seen, and felt deeply will all collude to keep us from holding the pose of structure. So why would I encourage you to *be the structure* when they may often resist it?

Because their resistance will most likely be a call for you to develop more pristine sensitivity and capacity in a few areas. First of all, you'll have to be sensitive enough to know if her resistance is useful feedback for your practice. Are you being meticulous? Are you weak-kneed in your sexual leadership? Are you questioning your own capacity? Are you being overly rigid? How is your breath? Posture? Your tone of voice? In many long-term and committed relationships, resistance can be traced to these areas 90 percent of the time. Can you playfully hold the pose for the sake of love? Often her initial resistance is simply a test. Are you for real? Are you going to be easily deterred? A woman needs to know these things before she opens her heart and trusts you with the most sacred spaces of her body, heart, and mind.

Recognize your feminine partner both as a sovereign being who can make her own decisions *and* as someone who desires to be taken beyond her own habitual, sexual, and emotional limitations for the sake of love.

Sometimes her resistance will indicate the need for in-the-moment adjustments for you to make that will allow your feminine partner to relax into letting you guide your time together. Other times her resistance will show you places in which your attention has been more on yourself than on what will serve love. Perhaps you haven't truly felt into her heart and what she can metabolize, and so you've pushed too fast, too soon. In this case, it's actually beautiful leadership to recognize where you may have gotten carried away. In fact, one of the most profound gifts you can offer a feminine partner is to feel where her genuine boundary is and hold it for her so that she doesn't have to.

It's a mistake to think that anyone who surrenders to Masculine leadership is somehow disempowering themselves. They are consciously choosing, for the sake of love, to amplify the sexual polarity possible in any given moment. It's an incredibly generous and powerful choice. And you should do it too. Whoever is the masculine partner in the moment, it's imperative that you recognize your feminine partner as both a sovereign being who can make their own decisions *and* as someone who desires to be taken beyond their own habitual, sexual, and emotional limitations for the sake of love. If you can't feel both, your partner has every reason to resist you. So, the less swayed you are by their willingness or resistance, the more they will trust you.

Your capacity to direct your relationship in the fields of time and space is just one type of offering. The integral structure of your physical and energetic body is actually more crucial, especially when you want to create an impactful moment. Her lack of trust can be a signal that your physical and energetic structure is lacking in some way. It can simply be a natural response to your slumping posture or shallow breath in the moment, or it may be that she's simply a *no* for some reason you've missed. Part of your responsibility as the masculine partner is to remain aware of the difference.

Is she a *no* to intimacy because other things (like work or family) are more important? Or is she a *no* because of how you're distracted or bunched up in some way that makes your leadership flaccid? She may not feel your depth and capacity to hold, cherish, and feel all of her. If that's the case, why wouldn't she be a *no*?

But the moment you straighten up and relax your heart, get out of your head, and really begin to feel her completely, your feminine partner's feelings may shift. A masculine being has to use his body, breath, and awareness as yogic tools to hold, guide, and circulate Feminine sexual energy, and he must present himself as trustable enough to take her someplace she can't take herself sexually. That's your value as the masculine partner in lovemaking. The opposite is of course her value. Accordingly, your posture needs to be strong, your breath full, and your presence both penetrating and healing. Your consciousness must be free to feel the entire field and space of relating and not be chained to rigid thoughts or agendas of how you want the sexual moment to go. This, of course, takes practice, feeling, and intention.

When your partner can sense that you have both felt and navigated the time and space of your relating, and she can feel the width and depth of your being, she can fully let go of any need to hold the structure. She can simply be the flow of energy and love that the structure you have created calls for.

Imagine you plan an evening together in which you have thought of absolutely everything. She is going to meet you at 9 p.m. The space you've prepared is impeccable. Great, right? The night is sure to be deeply loving and sexy.

Except you're lost in your own thoughts, you're breathing shallowly, you're ungrounded, you're not feeling your partner's heart or filling the space with your awareness. Regardless of the care you took to create the space, she is going to feel unheld, anxious, or annoyed. However, if you prepare the space with care and bring your deep breath, strong gaze, and feel into her heart, your feminine partner can relax and bring it all to you.

The dance of sexual polarity requires a moment-to-moment choice. Someone is always leading, directing, penetrating, and holding the sexual moment, while the other partner is peeling open, inviting, receiving, and surrendering into being love's ache and desire. One partner provides the structure and direction; the other reveals the full spectrum of love's bliss being deeply penetrated, seen, and held.

Physiology is the least powerful consideration when creating an arc of sexual polarity. There are deeper energetic exchanges that will create much more sublime and nourishing experiences. To this end, gender and sexual preference shouldn't be the deciding factors; *love* should decide. That's what transforms sex from mere pleasure-seeking to artful spiritual expression. Whose surrender is needed tonight for love to be most amplified? What dynamic most celebrates each partner's unique essence and touches the divine? Do the roles need to be skillfully alternated based on the moment-to-moment flow of energy?

For most couples, there's a clear desire for one partner to hold the Masculine most of the time, with the other partner preferring to be led, penetrated, and ravished most of the time. Other couples prefer moving back and forth frequently and agilely—or completely reversing the sexual poles altogether. It's a matter of personal exploration. But when lovers get confused about what their masculine or feminine essences truly desire, or they fall into the habit of chasing physical satisfaction, a subtle but chronic form of malnourishment begins to grow. After a few months or years, it becomes a chasm.

Whichever dynamic you choose, sexual polarity requires one partner giving the direction and the other partner surrendering into ecstasy and pleasure without having to decide what happens next. If both lovers are simultaneously telling each other what to do or both are trying to penetrate the other's heart, the sex will devolve into an energetic clash. I like the way Kundalini Yoga explains the optimal dynamic: one partner is the conscious giver while the other is the taker. This is how polarity works—it is a conscious decision to amplify the arc of energy by either taking control or surrendering control in the sexual moment. Dominants and submissives have practiced this yoga for years. Although gender politics have made sexual power dynamics a highly charged subject, most of us intuit that polarity is actually healthy when consciously and consensually enacted.

Yogic sexuality calls for whoever is holding the Masculine to fully and skillfully embody a grounded, heart-connected, and ruthlessly sacred form of command. This command can, of course, be silent—transmitted only through touch, gaze, and intention. Or it may come with self-assured directive language: *close your eyes, give me your hand,* or *come sit next to me, touch your thighs slowly, show me your neck.* What makes a command sacred is the masculine partner's steadfast commitment to love's primacy. He can feel what the feminine partner's body needs in order to relax and open and then use all manner of skill to take her there. He will know that the depth of his partner's ecstasy depends on how completely she can let go of the need to think, how fully she can surrender into trusting love, and how relaxed and open her body can become.

I'll recognize here that it's entirely normal for the Feminine to be apprehensive about this practice. Given the history of how men have controlled and even oppressed women over the centuries, that's understandable. However, when practiced within an impeccable container, the gifts in sexual intimacy are immeasurable. After talking to thousands of women on this subject, I'm convinced that in the moments of craving the deepest love, they are dying to be led into this type of profound and trustable sexual intimacy—beyond orgasm and the need for emotional security (and this is true for a man in his Feminine as well).

This depth of practice requires immense amounts of trust and sensitivity, so it should be entered into consciously, slowly, and gently—at least at first. It can be incredibly vulnerable to either take or completely surrender control, even with someone you truly love. And yet, this is the gesture in both directions that's required for the most sublime art. This capacity is what most of the practices in this book are training you to cultivate. It will take time, intention, and practice, but it will transform your sex life if you let it.

PRACTICE **WAKE UP YOUR BODY BEFORE SEX**

Take five minutes to crack open your body, slow down your nervous system, and bring energy more fully into your navel, genitals, and legs. Using one fist at a time, pound on both arms, the front and back of both legs, your torso, lower back, chest, and shoulders. Breathe deeply and intentionally sigh out any stress that is stuck in your muscles, tissues, and organs. Like breaking through a crust surrounding your body, methodically thump any areas of tension. Let the pounding wake up your body. Opening your physical form is necessary to feel and receive a partner more fully.

Next, plant your feet firmly on the ground, hip-width apart. Allow a slight bend in your knees. Straighten and elongate your spine. Soften your eyes. Take your right hand and place it on your lower belly just below the navel and breathe into the center of your palm.

Bringing all awareness to your breath as it moves slowly in and out; follow it down the front of your body into your lower abdomen and genitals. Gently exhale any tightness, worry, or stress—especially in the area around your heart. Take three minutes to connect to your breath in this way. It will quiet your mind, and your body will soften and open. In this state, take the last two minutes to set a strong, simple intention for lovemaking.

You can feel into your feminine partner in the next room and begin placing your attention on them. What is the state of their heart? What is their breathing like? What do you want them to feel? What turns you on about them? Can you bring some fierceness to your love and desire for them in this moment? From here, you can allow that desire to grow consciously in your belly and heart, and you can go to them with the iron-clad intention of claiming their heart and ravishing their body, in whatever way that arises in you.

If you are like most masculine beings, you will be able to access a depth and intensity that was, until now, elusive.

Learn to Pay Exquisite Attention
to Her Body Through Your Own

According to Deida, a quintessential desire of the Feminine is to be known and felt completely. She longs to have her heart fully seen, her body exquisitely felt and touched, and her soul penetrated and ravished. All of this occurs to her nervous system as the most sublime form of divine recognition. So, when your full body attention is on her and she can feel your heart's awareness, scan and caress every inch of her with your fingers, mouth, and eyes. She will naturally open to you in devotion because you are fulfilling a core need every feminine-identified being holds sacred.

The practice of bringing all your awareness to her body through your own is one of the most important sexual skills you can develop. It's a simple concept, but not easy to master, as we are prone to distraction (even during sex). Virtually all of the yogic breath and embodiment work I have presented in this book is meant to help you hone this capacity, but you must practice—and practice with her. Slow your breath, place your attention on the part of her you are touching, expand all five senses, and then pay attention to her body and heart.

Remember: the deepest experience you can bring in any relational moment is the combination of your complete awareness and feeling. This is the foundational practice throughout this book. It will amplify the pleasure and connection between you almost effortlessly. Don't just touch her skin—bring all of your awareness and feeling to your fingers as they caress her. Don't just kiss her—allow your lips and tongue to sense her mouth fully. Soften your heart, belly, and solar plexus, and witness her by exquisitely feeling her. You will notice an immediate depth arise in your connection, and you may even feel her receiving your love and attention more fully. And as you continue to breathe, move, and train your body more, you will become ever more attuned to new and beautiful parts of her that you may have missed or forgotten. So set your intention. The next time you are intimate with your lover, make your attention exquisite.

Create Space for Taboo and Her Dark Side

The subject of sexual taboo is layered and nuanced, and it deserves to be treated with profound reverence and respect. The yogic and tantric approach to creating space around sexual taboo treats both the emotional body and the sexual body through a lens of loving presence — allowing for what is rather than some homogenized notion of sexuality that *should* be.

Some taboos are born of childhood and adolescent wounds that often have very little to do with sex. Oftentimes, somewhere in our childhood or early adolescence, we explored sexuality or were sexualized in ways that evoked shame, confusion, punishment, or the threat of love's removal. Our young nervous systems, not knowing what to do with the conflicting messages, calcified around the amalgamation of turn-on, shame, and fear. These kinks lodged in our sexual bodies as a forbidden desire — a taboo.

The first step of taboo work is to simply own the desire.

An example I have seen repeatedly is that of a child who was spanked on their bare bottom as punishment by their mother or father. Depending on their age, the frequency of the contact, and the openness around early sexuality, the confusion and resulting taboo gets installed quite firmly in their nervous system. The emotional experience of being a "bad boy" or "bad girl" becomes sexually titillating, and it can be especially potent if the punishment was administered by the opposite-gendered parent. The child now grows into an adult who has an unowned sexual desire to be spanked, slapped, punished, and even humiliated.

Taboos are not exclusively physical. They can also spring from certain emotional malnourishments from childhood. If one parent withheld love or approval chronically, for example, the child might grow up seeking an older lover who holds similar archetypal energy. Or perhaps someone was turned on unexpectedly and innocently by an older sibling. The strongest taboos will often have a combination of excitement, shame, or even nausea attached to them. The details of their origins are less important than the combination of sensations, emotions, and beliefs that surround the taboos themselves. This is why the first step of taboo work is to simply own the desire—write it out, share it with trusted others, or bring it to light in some other way.

I want to be clear that there's not a damn thing wrong with these desires. We have little control over how we were raised, what and how we were taught about love, and how we were sexualized as children. However our bodies want to experience ecstasy is beautiful, as long as we don't injure or traumatize ourselves or others in the process. And so the second step of working with taboos is to hold them with consciousness and love, *especially* the darker and more often demonized taboos.

Even if the taboo isn't something we would ever consider following through with, the desire itself isn't bad or wrong. It deserves to be acknowledged, owned, and felt completely. It's crucial that we give space to our sexual darkness and find a way to work with the energy in a safe and loving container (most of the time, this can be done with no laws broken or marriages destroyed). Otherwise, we will close our bodies and nervous systems around the taboo and either repress massive amounts of sexual energy or feed it only with porn, fantasies, secret sexual lives, and perhaps even violence. This cycle of repression and acting out creates even more shame and tension in our hearts and bodies—to say nothing of the impact on those around us.

The third step in relating to our taboos is to consider what sexual energy and nourishment they offer us, because these energies are akin to specific nutrients that our nervous systems crave. For example, let's say that a college professor has a fantasy about being seduced by a group of young coeds. If we can get past the knee-jerk judgment of such a desire, we may find something quite innocent—the simple desire to be the recipient of vibrant and adoring sexual energy (a fairly common desire for masculine-identified humans). The imagined scene is just his mind's way to generate the possibility of that experience. Although trying to live out this fantasy with his students would be profoundly inappropriate, the desire expressed by the taboo isn't inappropriate at all—it's simply what his sexual nervous system craves.

Some women have taboo fantasies of being dominated sexually. What I have seen in many workshops over the years is the level of darkness women will express when given permission—kidnapping, multiple partners, and extremely rough sex—can be shocking. Underneath these fantasies, however, is the innocent desire to be taken, maybe even dominated into complete surrender, and the nutrients a woman receives when these taboos are held in heart-opened consciousness can be profound. Other women have fantasies of dominating their partners aggressively, or even of violence to men, and these taboos, too, feed a woman's soul in their own unique way, transcending something far greater than sexual gratification.

The shame that surrounds taboos almost always dissipates when the core desires are simplified and understood in this way. All that's left is the tenderness of human sexuality. People often feel empowered with this "unkinked" self-knowledge; it's freeing to truly recognize and own your fantasies.

The takeaway here is to craft your sex life with the loving recognition of what lies beyond your taboos and learn how to do the same for your lover. It's more than possible to artfully create scenarios in which one partner offers the other the yearned energy or archetype in the cradle of consciousness and love. Maybe she creates scenes of seduction during office hours, or he amplifies the energies of innocence or play in their sex. What might her partner do, feeling her unowned taboo about being lovingly dominated? Maybe they are more commanding in their sex or play out a scene of abduction for her?

This is how to take a more enlightened approach to taboo and explore who you need to become in order to live it out—either for yourself or for your partner. Who does each of you have to become to make this experience sacred? This exploration is, of course, meant to be done in a completely consensual, loving, and respectful container. What traits would a person have to embody in order to fully give themselves to a fantasy of abduction and domination? Surrender? A complete release of control? An abandonment to pleasure? Deep trust? In cultivating these traits or capacities, we come face-to-face with where our nervous systems reject or shut down certain parts of ourselves. When we were growing up, it was often not safe to fully surrender, and sometimes unequivocal trust was met with inconsideration or cruelty. Loss of control might have meant abandonment or harm. Whatever the case, it's a true challenge to train your body to go into these places and learn otherwise. The truth is, these traits and capacities—to surrender, to trust, to let go completely in the very ways your taboo is asking you to show up—are the very capacities the world is craving from you as well.

Our taboos often hold the key to how we can become more available to those we would love, serve, and inspire. Accepting and appreciating our fantasies isn't just about getting off or having some superficial hunger filled; it's about becoming someone more available to love. It's a practice of opening to give, receive, and discover more of yourself in service to something greater. It is ultimately about consciousness and love.

Know What Nourishes Her Sexually

It's critical to pay ongoing attention to what nourishes your feminine partner sexually. It's far too easy to get stuck in habits of lovemaking that worked in the past or get hung up on notions of performance. Your value as a sexual partner is to know her heart and body so keenly that you can feel what's most nourishing to her in the moment, as well as long term.

Every human's sexual imprint is different, and what nourishes you very well might not be the same for her. Or it may change over time. Developing a keen attunement of her body's evolving needs is an act of supreme love. Does she get fed by tenderness? Or does she need to feel the darker, fiercer, more defiling part of you? Does she need to be commanded sexually? Or encouraged to tell you what feels good? Feel beyond her preferences or habits and into her actual needs.

To use a food analogy, she may love sweets, but what her body actually needs is iron and calcium. If all you give her is one kind of nutrient over and over again, don't be surprised when part of her becomes malnourished. If your sex is always wild, rough, and spontaneous, maybe she needs a night of planned lovemaking that's slow, gentle, and devotional. If you always make love with the lights out, maybe being fully seen with loving eye contact will nourish her body. Try something new and be willing to fail. Pay attention before, during, and after sex as to whether her heart and body are responding. This is an important aspect of leading sexually.

Bring awareness and skill to what is needed. Get curious, investigate, and ask her questions. When is she most turned on? Did she like it when you pulled her hair? Were you too rough, or not rough enough? Find out for yourself and begin to craft experiences that heal, nourish, and awaken dormant or under-expressed parts of her—her wildness, devotion, aggressiveness, or innocence. There are thousands of possibilities. Sex is the art of expressing love and seeking divine union, and as such, it shouldn't be limited to one color palate or texture. Learning how to encourage, evoke, and nourish a wide range of what is possible is what will make you an artist.

Develop Masculine *and* Feminine Sexual Capacities

As Deida teaches, your freedom to dynamically play in reciprocal loving across the full masculine and feminine sexual range is a key to sublime and life-changing sex. In vulnerable attunement with each other, one partner relaxes as ever-present depth while the other more animates life's fullness. Again, gender isn't the defining factor here. It's about one partner inviting and one partner penetrating. One brings the energy and love light; the other offers depth and structure. One ravishes; the other is ravished. One practices yearning while the other practices filling the yearning with conscious love. Polarities amplify sexual energy like positive and negative charges of electricity or magnetic energy.

Most of us are aware that we have both masculine and feminine sides; it's just that we don't normally use them consciously. I had to train myself to become more aware of sexual structure, depth, and leadership and then choose to animate them as a sexual gift. But I also had to learn to become more vulnerable and expressive and develop sensitivity to my own body, as well as my partner's. To generate, move, receive, and ultimately share my pleasure fully. To allow myself to be ravished. To allow her to see and receive my pleasure. To be penetrated by her love. Cultivating both polar capacities took time and separate modalities of practice.

Practicing both sides of the sexual energetic coin also helps us develop sexual and energetic agility and sensitivity. It allows us as men to be tender and open-hearted in one moment and fierce and commanding the next. Cultivating the feminine sexual gifts of vulnerability, pleasure, yearning, and energetic flow in our bodies also allows us to feel more, receive more, and understand our lover's needs and desires more. If you allow yourself to cultivate yearning and pleasure in your body, you become more fully alive—not just genitally stimulated. That aliveness translates into you feeling more, her feeling you more, and just becoming a more sensitive lover overall.

> Make connection, pleasure, depth, and love
> your intention—not just getting off.

The best way to practice this is to take turns. One night you be the present, piercing, embodied consciousness that deepens and holds the sex while she practices being the blossoming invitation, receptivity, love, and pleasure. You animate desire as depth, structure, and awareness while she animates the yearning and pleasure as energy through her body. On the next night, switch. Allow her to penetrate you either physically, energetically, or both. Relax into receiving her consciousness and love. Let the front of your body bloom open. Let your heart be slightly broken by it. Practice being ravished and allowing it. Receive her desire into the center column of your body—into your heart and spine.

This interplay can manifest in oral sex, fondling, kissing, or full-on penetration. As you develop this agility, you will notice a greater level of feeling, expanse, and possibility. You will be able to go farther in each direction, and ultimately your moments of polarized sexual union will deepen profoundly.

Practice Goalless Sex

In addition to leading artful lovemaking into more energetic agility for both of you, it's beneficial to let go of any notion of completion in sex altogether. Let go of orgasm being the end-all goal for either of you. Make connection, pleasure, depth, and love your intention—not just getting off. The irony here is that when all the pressure is removed and the emphasis is on feeling and pristine attention, orgasms come more naturally.

This allows for a deeper exploration into the yoga and meditation of sex—the art of pleasure and devotion. The more you focus on the journey into each other's hearts and bodies, the more free, intense, and filled with pleasure your sex will become. How far into the polarities of structure and flow, consciousness and love, masculine and feminine can you go? How much pleasure, connection, and sexual energy can you train your body to hold and circulate? How deeply can you penetrate her body and heart from your core? These are all capacities that will make you a stronger, more sensitive, and more capable human. They will also heal and nourish her.

Honor Her *No*—Love Her Resistance

On one hand, men intuit that women crave masculine boldness and confidence. They've heard that a romantic partner wants to be deftly taken, claimed, and deeply ravished. But they're also aware in today's world that attempting to do so without a partner's clear and expressed consent is immoral and abusive. Men have trouble understanding issues of consent—especially nonverbal consent—and women are understandably weary of having to educate them and explain themselves. It's crucial that men and women get on the same page with this, because the *no* issue certainly is a substantial and pernicious one.

I want to suggest another way—one that can both engender trust *and* create sexual spark. Men can absolutely learn to notice and feel what's happening in a feminine partner's body, and they can train their nervous systems to feel past their own desires and home in on her cues, some of which she may not even be aware of. She may hold her breath, tense her shoulders, or clench her belly as you move closer. The muscles of her jaw or around her heart might tighten up or soften depending on how much she trusts you at that moment. A man can become a master at understanding this real form of nonverbal communication if he can relax his body, deepen his breath, and learn to feel beyond his own thoughts and desires. And so, learning the difference between a true *no*, a temporary closure, and what Feminine embodiment teacher Kendra Cunov calls a "not yet or not like that" is a necessary skill to learn as a masculine partner.

There are three primary *noes* in intimacy with a feminine partner. One is a sacred *no*—usually the by-product of an intuitive knowing—and often with regard to you in a relational or sexual moment. Whether on a second date or in a twenty-year marriage, this *no* is meant to be fully honored and taken as a piece of serious feedback, because it emerges directly from the wisdom of her body. It indicates that something isn't right and that you need to back off and take a good look at yourself. She doesn't trust you for some reason. Maybe you're not present or fully conscious; you could be distracted, emotionally incongruent, or even breathing shallowly; perhaps you're drinking too much or numbing out excessively via television or the Internet; you could very well be insensitive to her needs; your touch may be unconscious, piggish, or needy; you could be obsequious, too focused on receiving her approval, or caught up in trying to make her happy at all costs. Whatever the source of her deep *no*, it's a warning sign. And it's a gift from her heart.

Well, it's a gift as long as you have the humility, strength of character, and nervous system stability to receive it. That sort of feedback requires reflection, honesty, awareness, and the ability to take action according to what the moment calls for. If she is a *no* more often than a *yes*, it's definitely time to ask yourself what's going on. It's usually not that hard to find out why her heart is closed to you—if you really look, if you really feel into it. Chances are she wants to be a *yes* to you—that's why she chose you in the first place. So, what's stopping her?

Your work is to ferret out the disconnection and forge a return to integrity. Your capacity to receive this feedback and use it to better yourself will pay remarkable dividends in your intimacy, your work, and elsewhere in your world. Whatever she sees in you is also visible to others; they just don't reflect it back as clearly.

There's another kind of *no*, and it presents a different sort of challenge. Oftentimes this *no* shows up as a bad mood, petty criticism, or ongoing resentment. It may be an insecurity she's projecting onto you or a grudge from a previous fight. Or she may have just had a shitty day. This kind of mood-driven *no* is like a passing weather pattern that most men confuse as something more substantial and solid.

In fact, this kind of *no* can be a call to be liberated from the shitstorms of life and be skillfully led back into the essence of love by a partner she trusts. Consider this as her desire to tussle. It's an opportunity for you to use your depth, play, and presence to pierce her heart and help her remember that you love all of her—even the childish or downright scornful parts of her—and that you aren't going to collapse in the face of those passing aspects. If you can do so, it will occur to the feminine nervous system as grounding and sexually energizing. It creates a massive amount of trust in you, because she called out in pain and you answered.

Misunderstanding their partner's moods is the one of the most significant missed opportunities I see from men in their relationships. The next time this happens for you, instead of recoiling in hurt, try smiling, teasing her for being sassy, or kissing her on the neck. If she giggles or softens, you'll know you're on the right track. If she doesn't, it will be a sign that something more substantial is going on. Either way, train your nervous system to weather her moods and feel if she wants to be loved or left alone. Consider that her mood has little to do with you, and remember that you are fully empowered to bring her home to love.

Of course, there is a third type of *no* that is much more tricky to navigate, and that's the *no* that arises from her mistrust of intimacy. If she did not receive love and care from a trustable masculine presence in her childhood, of course it will show up in your relationship. Remember that many of her *noes*—and yours as well—are unwound habits or impulses of childhood programming and don't emanate from the present-moment flow of love. Many humans reject love for all kinds of reasons, most of which are unconscious. This is an incredibly important place you can guide her into her heart. You can help her navigate these places of mistrust by showing your capacity to not give up on love.

The essential gift of the Masculine is to feel what is needed most in any dynamic from a place of open, rested consciousness and then to liberate those involved with right action, sourced from depth. This is how you can allow her to relax into her Feminine at any moment, because she knows you've got *it*—whether that *it* is about disciplining your child, deciding where you're going to spend the weekend, or what comes next in your lovemaking. That being said, if you've read this far, you'll know better than to be surprised when she meets you with some mistrust.

Looked at in this way, it's quite normal for her to test your capacity to stay open in the midst of her resistance or downright refusal when it comes to your attempts at leadership. And remember that she may have every reason to do so—generations of abuse, a history of neglect, or years and years of suffering from sexual manipulation. She may also be accustomed to control and making all of the decisions herself. And if she has previously handled all of the family's finances and parenting choices, or unconsciously been forced to be in charge of initiating sex, it's going to take some skill and commitment on your part while her nervous system adjusts to the changes. Of course, leading well also means knowing, admitting, and giving her space to lead in areas in which she is more capable than you are.

The truth is that many women today are way more capable of leading than men are—spiritually, emotionally, and even financially. This puts pressure on them to step into the role of leading in all aspects of their lives if they want to get anything done—but that level of control comes at a price. Some women want their partners to take over more of the leadership, but they don't trust that they'll want to do so, know how to follow through, or even do a decent job of it. So, why wouldn't they hold on to all of that control?

But for a masculine partner who wants the life-changing kind of sexual intimacy, it's crucial that he not allow his partner to suffer spending massive amounts of time and energy in her Masculine unless she expressly says she wants to. He therefore must make the commitment to take hold of this sacred charge: it is the single most important premise of this book.

She may not trust you to lead her better than she can lead herself, and yet she will likely resent you if you don't. You may not want to add the burden of taking responsibility for her body, mind, and heart in your moments of intimacy to your ever-growing list of things to master in your life, but so much is riding on it. Everything transformative, revolutionary, and mind-blowingly ecstatic is riding on it.

PRACTICE INVESTIGATING HER *NOES*

Take the next week to reflect on how her *noes* show up in your relationship. Can you distinguish the underlying textures of feeling that lie below each of them? Consciously engage your awareness and feeling-body to attune to her resistance, rejections, and outright *noes*. Reflect not only on the various ways your partner responds to your lack of consciousness but also on how she gets yanked out of her love-essence by tasks and duties. Also take a look at her resistance even to your most sincere and loving attempts at leading her in your sexual and relational intimacy.

After you've spent a couple of weeks monitoring this *no* dynamic, sit down and have an honest conversation about where you would love to lead more powerfully. How could you relieve her of some of the burdens she carries? How could you bring more vitality and fullness to your intimacy? What is she missing in her personal life that would make her more open and filled with love? Does she need extra time for yoga or spending time with her friends? Does she need to set firmer boundaries about the time she spends at work? Don't be afraid to step in and help her by being the masculine presence in the relationship every now and then—especially when you know that would serve her. Finally, ask her what she would need to trust your leadership more. Her answer will be critical to your growth.

Create Expansive and Connective Sexual Practices and Rituals

Artistry in relationships and in sex requires practice, rituals, and intentions to expand what is possible for you both sexually and emotionally. As I've said before, the masculine gift in the relationship is the awareness, structure, and clarity that makes your sexual connection its most profound. This means that if you detect that something needs attention in your relationship—more variety in sex, for example, or more attention to touch—then you need to take the lead. Don't make her do it. Don't force her to take on even more of the masculine role.

Create whatever structure it takes for her to relax and bring the full force of her energy, love, and pleasure. This needs to go beyond simply playing out fantasies or planning date nights. Your awareness as to what is truly needed to liberate more love between you will require real, ongoing, disciplined attention. If you feel the two of you are disconnected in sex, it's up to you to create a practice addressing it—for example, staring into each other's eyes while you enter her slowly and not breaking the gaze until you melt into each other's hearts. Or if you've both been under a lot of stress due to outside pressures or physical separation, make a ritual of recommitting to each other—a tea ceremony, a silent evening making dinner together, tying a ribbon around both of your wrists as a gesture of bonding, or simply taking turns touching each other for thirty minutes with no agenda other than offering pleasure and love.

Real romance is less about fancy dinners and vacations, and more about intentional connection and sustained, authentic relating.

Make Praise and Worship an Essential Part of Your Sex

Praise is the doorway to worship. To praise another person is to deeply honor their humanity. When we praise another, we turn our awareness to what is exquisite about them, and we honor who they uniquely are in the world. When you commit to a consistent praise practice, you are signing on to honor the best your partner has to offer, and your articulated witnessing will evoke even more of that from them.

If you want to transform your relationship, prioritize praising each other's sex, generosity, warmth, and commitment to love. Make praise an art. Learn to do it with exactly the right tone and precisely the right time, noticing the gesture or trait your partner is longing to have acknowledged. Praise at every opportunity, especially when you don't want to. It will rewire your nervous system, open your heart, and train your mind to see what is right in your lover in ever newer and deeper ways.

> Worship allows us to see through a person's transient characteristics and behavior and feel into their true nature.

While praise is a beautiful and invaluable relational practice, worship will unveil an even deeper source of love, awe, and devotion available at any moment. Worship is the practice of seeing past the human surface of your partner into the unchanging and eternal nature of existence. To worship another person is to embody devotion to the essential divine in them. In worship, we turn our awareness to the Infinite within their human form. Within the framework of spiritual intimacy and yogic sexuality, we worship the essential unchanging nature of consciousness—what we refer to as the Masculine—and we worship the constantly shifting flow of love within—the Feminine.

It's all too easy to come up with reasons why we don't want to worship a particular partner, and usually those reasons have to do with childhood wounds or those of prior relationships. But worshiping the deepest place in them is a timeless practice, free from the binds of our past, and a practice that requires our commitment to the divine. What's beneath her surface is infinite heart-space, filled with love. What's beneath his appearance is a form of consciousness as wide and endless as the cosmos. Worship allows us to see through a person's transient characteristics and behavior and feel into their true nature.

Training our awareness to penetrate into these sacred spaces is as much a spiritual practice as reciting a sutra or repeating the rosary. It's how we see God (whatever you call God) in each other, as well as ourselves.

LEARNING TO LEAD
AND INTEGRATE
YOUR OWN FEMININE

Holding Your Own Feminine

All of our thoughts, feelings, sensations, emotional states, and habits are movements of our own Feminine display. Hearing this from Deida was a revelation for me, as I came to understand that I would have to learn to shepherd, hold, and ultimately accept my own emotions, feelings, desires, fears, and insecurities. You will have to learn this as well if you want to have integrity as a masculine partner. This means learning to create structures and practices to process and integrate them. You will need to take responsibility for your own human experience and become artful at owning, moving, and expressing it—or you and others will suffer from your projections. In short, no one is going to trust your leadership unless you've got a handle on your own Feminine.

To that end, you have to learn to lead yourself through the often turbulent and challenging landscape of your own heart and nervous system. As men, we must take full responsibility for our states of being, or we will get knocked over by the winds of life that gust at the most unexpected times. We must get clear and give space for our needs and desires. We need to own and cultivate our capacity to hold, love, and guide ourselves into more authentic and powerful truths without any withholding or collapse. All of the explorations and practices in this section are meant to help you artfully and compassionately dance with your Feminine.

I see far too many men struggle with fully owning their needs and desires, although both are healthy and natural. The part of you that craves space and freedom to escape responsibility; the part of your heart that longs for love and recognition; the parts that crave certain forms of sexual energy, and so on. Whatever it is, the part of you that yearns, desires, and needs is your Feminine. And this part of your nature needs to be nurtured and expressed without judgment. If you don't allow these yearnings in yourself, you'll more than likely have a problem with them in other people—including the ones you love.

Lots of humans have the tendency to clamp down on their desires and needs for fear that they will appear needy, lose the love and attention of those close to them, or be shamed and rejected. But the real weakness when it comes to desires and needs isn't in having them but in *not owning them*, not taking responsibility for communicating them, not creating a culture that supports them, and not holding and guiding those beautiful parts of yourself. Whatever your yearning, part of shepherding your own Feminine is honoring it as if it were the holy and most precious desire of someone you resolutely care about.

So, get curious about your needs and desires. Consider them sacred. Create space for them. Shepherd them. Discover how you can fully own and express them. Just as you would encourage your child or lover to own and honor their yearnings, you need to do like-wise for yourself.

If you have a need for solitude in nature, then make that clear to your partner and those who rely on you and schedule alone time in nature. If you need a certain kind of love — affection, devotion, or intense sexual energy — it is yours to own and clearly communicate. Your desires are just fine as they are. They're an integral aspect of your humanity.

Good masculine leadership means creating a space for needs and desires without allowing them to transform into damaging projections or addictions. For example, if you want more devotion from your feminine partner, you can own that by saying, "My love, I long to feel less drive and stress from you, and more care and attention to me and to us." That's clear ownership of a desire. But if you instead let it manifest as constant criticism, or you allow that unmet need to fester and then explode in an angry and accusatory tirade, then you've allowed your natural desire to turn into something destructive.

Remember that the Feminine in all of us can take the form of life-giving or life-destroying energy. It can either be the flower of love or the volcano of rage. So, your capacity to reveal, modulate, and clearly express what's in your heart is a key component of your own masculine capacity for self-leadership, as well as leadership in your relationships.

Like many men, I've struggled with addictions and compulsions. Whether it's food, sex, drugs, booze, or video games, the Feminine in all of us craves more of what feels good. Those impulses, when left unchecked, can derail your best attempts at presence, purpose, and living from the core. The pull of distractions and comfort is surprisingly pervasive and strong. I'm not saying you shouldn't drink, smoke, or play

Call of Duty until three in the morning—that's for you to decide and reflect on. But I will say that a significant aspect of leading yourself is in understanding how your own Feminine nature arises as both beautiful longings and unhealthy impulses. And then your work will be to accentuate what liberates more love while creating healthy boundaries for those parts that can be destructive.

Knowing that my cell phone is often a distractive draw on my attention, I bought a timed lockbox. Whenever I need to give something my total focus, I put my phone in the lockbox for a certain period of time—usually somewhere between two and ten hours—and I try to forget about it. That's my way of creating a structure to work with the part of me that wants to check email and social media compulsively. Other structures to work with addictions include twelve-step programs, men's groups, and psychotherapy. Choose something that works for you, but understand that these parts of you that want such things have always been okay in themselves and are utterly natural. They don't need to be eradicated. They just need guidance to help you live in healthier and more constructive ways.

> Most of us men have been taught to ignore or cover
> over our wounds in the name of productivity.

On the other end of the Feminine spectrum are the traits of nurturing, sensitivity, receptivity, intuition, and our ability to move energy. Cultivating these places in you will make you stronger and more magnetic. Leading these places in you requires making commitments to cultivate them, recognizing their irreplaceable value, and artfully sharing them with those you love. So much of this work is about fostering these places in yourself and then using the masculine tools of clarity, direction, and consciousness to apply them to life. Set aside time to practice what makes you more sensitive—for example, tai chi, qigong, dance, or some form of nonlinear movement. Create sexual and meditative practices to become more receptive to whatever it is that life wants to give you. Cultivate intuition by learning to feel in the moment.

Here's a practice I do often myself and give to men in my groups. Find time each day to just sit—preferably in nature—and do nothing but receive what the moment wants to give you. It could be an emotion, a hit about a business or creative challenge, or just the raw nourishment of life. But make that sitting time a sacred place for you to have to *do* nothing but receive the nuances of the present moment. Do nothing, meticulously and consciously. Let the mysteries of life arise in the stillness.

One important area of our Feminine nature that requires more attention is our thoughts. Most of us engage in habitual thought loops that just seem to arise out of nowhere. We can't control how these thoughts pop up, but we can train our awareness to create space around them and guide them into more productive states of being. The idea is to simply witness them without boarding the train and letting them haul us around indiscriminately. One of our lifelong masculine practices, and one that meditative traditions have sought to address for centuries, is to allow thoughts to arise while still retaining some steering capacity, all while engaging in the awareness to see how our thought patterns affect us and those around us. To do so, we need to rely on the structure of breath and our honed awareness to hold and guide them, which—let's be honest—can sometimes be a real bear.

The better you become at owning and embodying your own Feminine, the more whole you become (and the more trustable as an integral leader). You'll also learn to hold, nurture, and celebrate the Feminine in those around you.

Do Your Own Deep Work

Your capacity as a true leader—be it in love, business, or your community—will require others to feel that you have faced your own wounds and demons squarely. If you truly want to inspire trust in those around you, you have to go into your heart and soul and face death, so to speak. Look at your greatest fears, your most painful wounds, your most pernicious insecurities, and your habits of addiction and disconnection.

Feel them, address them, and bring them out into the light. Use the men around you to honestly reveal how much you truly struggle. Rather than trying to hide your flaws from others, face them and turn them into allies on your journey. That's what it takes to be a true leader. That's the journey that will free you and those around you.

The Buddhist teacher Pema Chödrön regularly tells her students to become "unconditionally friendly" to their most wounded places, and she encourages them to look at feeling deeply as a form of conscious warrior-ship. Most of us men have been taught to ignore or cover over our wounds in the name of productivity, perhaps because many of our ancestors faced constant hardships and ongoing food and security issues. But most of us today don't have to deal with the same challenges, and so we can afford to turn our hearts and minds to the very clear need for emotional integrity. We must become unconditionally friendly with our wounded parts; we must acknowledge and lovingly hold our pain. If we don't, it will invariably leak out to those we love and hurt those who call out for our benevolent leadership. Begin this lifelong friendship today, by organizing a time to fully be with these parts of you, simply and intentionally.

PRACTICE WRITING OUT YOUR FEARS

Set aside thirty minutes or more to reflect on your most substantial fears and wounds. What insecurities continually pop up? What is your current response when you feel fear? Pain? Stress? Write down the ways that these show up in your relationships. What roles do fear and your wounding play in the areas of relationship that are least satisfying to you? How do you deal with these experiences? Where do you numb out with escapism, addiction, or comfort? Finally, think about what you can do to face and heal these fears and wounds. Imagine what your life would look like if you were free of these painful feelings. Who would you be? How would your relationships change?

Working with (and Overcoming) Fear

You've probably heard that the antidote to fear is love, and that's absolutely true. But how love flows through the body, where the pulse of love lives, and what constitutes the energy of love are all topics that are widely misunderstood. What might it mean to overcome fear with love?

Let's think of love as an awakened energetic quality that we can actually attune to, amplify, and wield moment to moment in our lives. It could be the love for another or the energized experience of being alive. The cultivation of chi or prana in the body also occurs to us as a form of love. We can surrender to it—as in a moment of profound passion—and let it take over our bodies and hearts. This flow of energy moves through the heart, but that's not the only place love lives or comes from.

There's the love we generate by paying attention to someone we care about or putting our all into some activity we adore, but there's a different kind of love that hits us out of nowhere and brings us to tears or makes our chest feel as if it's about to burst. With this kind of love, you didn't necessarily *do* anything. It just arrives, like a gift. And your unexpecting body simply becomes a vessel for an incredibly powerful transmission.

The life-changing truth that we too often miss is that connecting to love is a physical act as much as it is an emotional one, and our bodies can take the shape of love's transmission or flow at any time. We can lift our hearts a half-inch higher. We can open our solar plexus and make it more available. We can soften our gaze, our eyes, and our throats. We can take deeper breaths. All of these adjustments are like tuning the physical transmitter of your heart to a universal source of power greater than any fear.

Another option is to simply breathe and move, following the innate wisdom of how and where your body wants to take in air and where it wants to travel on each exhale. As you relax, allow, and receive, your corporal wisdom will begin to move and open you. This form of nonlinear movement I learned from movement teacher Cass Phelps is a more feminine style of practice that can align you with the flow of love permeating life at all times. You may become emotional, shudder, or make the guttural sounds of your body's unwinding. But keep going and allow your body to move and open as love.

There are countless other ways to help your body receive and conduct love—reminding yourself of what you're grateful for, for example, or looking at yourself in the mirror and saying, "I love the tender, young part of me that is afraid." Just know that the most profound and powerful streams of love are visceral experiences in the body, not the mind. Overcoming stubborn feelings of fear simply requires us to tap into the stream of love, because it entails infinitely more energy than any thought forms we could have, including those we call fear.

> Our perceptual and cognitive systems are biased to only take in and process external data that suits our worldview.

Own and Transmute Your Negative Beliefs

We all have a set of core beliefs that filter our thoughts, run undetected in the background, impact our actions, and regularly contribute to closures in our hearts and bodies. Quite often, we don't even know that they are driving our moods, decisions, and worldviews. They are pernicious, sneaky, and often rooted in mistaken or constricted notions of reality—and, in truth, they are what carry our ideas of ourselves, other people, and the world forward into future encounters. Some examples include *everything is a struggle* and *I'm never enough* and *I fuck everything up*. It's fairly easy to see how believing such things would impact your quality of life and ultimately your destiny.

Most of these beliefs came from early childhood programming based on what we did or didn't receive from our parents, and they were installed in our nervous systems by often well-meaning, but unconscious, caregivers. As we moved through life, these beliefs were enhanced or encouraged in our experiences with lovers, friends, employers, relatives, teachers, the media, and so on, and it doesn't take too many years of this dynamic to fully convince us that our beliefs are utterly and infallibly true.

All of us are predisposed to certain beliefs in this way. Furthermore, our perceptual and cognitive systems are biased to only take in and process external data that suits our worldview. If you believe that your neediness is repulsive and unattractive, you will more than likely find people to confirm that for you—either by only seeking out certain types of romantic partners, for example, or endlessly interpreting their reactions to your needs in a particular way. Your lover might be trying to communicate otherwise, but you diminish or dismiss their attempts without even recognizing that you're doing so.

The problem isn't necessarily that we have these beliefs; the problem is that we aren't aware of them. Awareness allows us to create some space around them, examine their persistent truth claims, and even transmute them into beliefs that actually serve us and our relationships.

As other practices in this book indicate, your awareness is the key to changing your behavior. The first step is to know what the belief is—make it conscious, articulate it, and see how it plays out in your life with clarity and compassion. Once you are able to do this, the next task is to investigate whether or not the belief has any merit. To this end, trusted friends or therapists can prove tremendously helpful. As you discover that a particular belief may not actually be true, you can begin to consider alternatives—for example, instead of thinking *others view my neediness as weakness*, you could choose something more suitable to the facts, such as *my tender heart is a gift*.

Our ability to transmute beliefs in this way is so straightforward and simple that most people have trouble believing it's possible (perhaps due to another core belief—for example, *everything worthwhile is always too hard for me*). With awareness and some discipline, you can actually choose what you want to believe and then practice it, over and over, until your heart and nervous system can integrate it and create a whole new reality for you. The key is to continually refine and upgrade your belief systems for ones that actually benefit you and others. Before you can do this though, you have to get clear on what your current belief systems are and how they are running in your life. The following is a powerful practice to help you identify these beliefs and shift them toward your desired experience.

PRACTICE **YOUR OCCURRING WORLD**

Pick a belief that has dogged you throughout your life or one that's particularly active at this time. It might be something like "money is scarce" or "relationships are too much work." Whatever the belief, shine the light of your awareness on it completely. Notice how and where your whole world has "occurred" that way.

Write down your reflections and examine how this belief has cost you in your life. What have you missed or sabotaged because of it? How much tension and stress does it cause you or others you love? Who is no longer in your life because of it? Or what opportunities did you squander? Take a minute to really feel the consequences of your chosen occurring world belief. Don't shy away from it; feel everything bravely as a warrior might.

Next, find an opposing, more empowering belief. To contrast the above examples, it might be something like "money comes easily to me" or "relationships bring me joy and ease." Write down all of the ways these beliefs could be just as true, and note examples from your life where you have seen these polar beliefs play out but perhaps have habitually ignored them in favor of their negative versions.

Finally, breathe these new empowering possibilities into your heart for three full minutes. Envision them, feel them, and let them roll around in your head like new destiny-changing mantras. Notice how your nervous system relaxes and accepts the new beliefs. Continue breathing in and reaffirming them as part of your daily practice for a week. Notice if these new beliefs begin to manifest for you in powerful and unexpected ways.

Let Your Anger Turn to Anguish

Anger is a natural aspect of life, whether it has to do with our partners, parents, or the state of the world. Anger can be essential in cultivating the emotional integrity that our partners crave, and sometimes it's the only thing that will wake our partners up. To deny our anger is to deny a fundamental part of what it means to be human.

And yet, when anger is our dominant mode, we too often miss out on the more tender and vulnerable emotions that make life worth living. Furthermore, when we don't own and channel our anger appropriately, it can be a destructive force. Most of the time, our anger is tied more to past wounds and traumas than to what's currently in front of us, and our outbursts seem to be our only way to deal with all of the fear, grief, powerlessness, and so on that we feel inside but have no idea how to process. For this reason, it's crucial that we learn how to express our anger in connective ways that reveal the truths of our hearts.

Making your anger an ally in your relationships requires you to first own your anger, as well as the more tender emotions that your anger may be trying to protect. Anguish is one emotion that almost always lies just beneath the surface—anguish for the fear we've been carrying, anguish for unprocessed grief, anguish for long-held desires gone unrealized.

You've probably seen people move from rage to vulnerable tears in a matter of seconds. There's a moment when our heart softens in the midst of anger and makes space for our anguish to arise. One minute we're outraged and yelling at our partner; the next, our eyes are full of tears and our hearts are cracked open. No matter how difficult the anger was to express and experience, these are the moments that draw partners instantly together—energetically and emotionally. This is the power of revealing your anguish.

Not that it's easy, of course. Most of us were never taught how to do so, and more often than not we were actually encouraged to believe that our grief and anger are a problem (no wonder so many of us guard our hearts so tightly). Accessing and expressing our anguish takes tremendous courage and ongoing practice, but—unlike voicing anger—revealing our anguish, grief, and fear has a tendency to heal and strengthen relationships. The following is a short practice for you to try the next time you feel anger rising up during an argument or otherwise tense situation.

PRACTICE BREATHING INTO ANGUISH

Take a few deep breaths and let each exhale relax the muscles in and around your heart and chest. Bring your awareness to the emotions and sensations that lie underneath your rage (these are almost always unmet desires, fears, or needs from our childhood). If you're already hot with anger, let it flow directly from your heart, as opposed to your head. Keep breathing and relaxing in and around your heart—eventually, the anger will soften. It may only take thirty seconds, or it might take thirty minutes—keep going no matter what. Let yourself connect to your feelings of anguish and feel the longing in your heart. Allow others to witness you in this vulnerable and beautiful state, and then—in two or three sentences—express what the tender spot in your heart wants to say ("I feel so alone when you ignore me," for example, or "I feel so sad and hopeless when you criticize me"). Note the profound difference this kind of simple, heartfelt, vulnerable expression can make.

Feel What You Have Been Avoiding

Consistently ask yourself what feelings you're avoiding. Are there childhood traumas, old heartbreaks, family griefs, or unprocessed losses that you haven't created the time and space to feel completely? Have you thrown yourself into your work and worldly success rather than feel the depth of grief at the loss of a meaningful relationship? Have you addressed the heartache of a parent's rejection? What ancient pain is still alive in you? Most of us carry some kind of emotional scar tissue beneath the surface, and if you've ever had a proficient bodyworker dig in with their knuckles and elbows to break up and move physical scar tissue, you know it can hurt like crazy.

It took me until my early forties to truly grieve the absence of my father in the way I needed and craved him (and this was after a decade of focusing on the topic). Growing up, I wasn't taught how to take care of money. I wasn't shown how to love a woman with integrity. I had no idea how to be a guiding presence for my family or how to be a powerful and benevolent man in the world. All I knew was that I was full of grief, loneliness, and rage. Luckily, I had a men's group that could help me identify and move these feelings. They could see that it was negatively affecting my relationships, especially with men. And as a would-be leader in the field of men's work, this particular excavation was crucial for me to attend to.

Whatever the feeling, experience, or repressed emotion, doing your own deep work requires a warrior's intention to dive into your history to find the threads that need to be pulled apart. Be honest with yourself and at least one other good friend. Once you have identified something that calls out to be examined, dive in and make a personal ritual of the process: set the intention to feel and transmute whatever has been hidden or suppressed, play inspiring music, and create a special place for the ritual. For a while, I had a garage office I would go into for thirty minutes or so if I needed to get in touch in this way. For some, men's groups help with this type of work, too.

When you do this with courage and commitment, you may feel a lot more freedom, energy, space, and openness. It can actually feel as if a heavy weight has been removed from your heart. The quality of your relationships will change. Even if you have been with someone for years who hasn't fully appreciated your love, using this practice to touch the grief you feel about it will foster more intimacy, connection, and gratitude. And it's undoubtedly a lot easier to own your needs and hold your head high when you aren't sitting on a backlog of unexpressed emotions.

Don't Compromise Your Heart's Core Truths

The masculine practice of integrity has as much to do with knowing your own heart as it does with keeping your word. Once you have done the work to own your core truths, don't let anyone compromise them—not the people you work with, not your parents, not your romantic partners. If you've done what it takes to know your core desires, wounds, and truths, trust what you've found and dive in, whether it means quitting your job to go surf the world or sharing with trusted others the core fear that stops you from keeping your heart open. Your truth is yours. No one can take it from you. Own it proudly and communicate it kindly. Those around you will sense your integrity and alignment—and they will either trust you more because of it and become inspired, or they will leave. Either way, you'll live more fully with the clarity and power that comes from taking a stand from the core of your heart.

> Knowing your truths doesn't require you
> to bludgeon the world with them.

This often will require difficult conversations with people you love dearly. Maybe one or both of you have been compromising a part of you that shouldn't be compromised. Maybe one of you needs to be polyamorous, or needs way more alone time, or doesn't want to have children after all, or needs more affection and sexual attention, or needs to quit their job and travel the world and write poetry. Whatever it is, being in true integrity with yourself means establishing integrity in your relationships, and that's often a lot easier said than done.

Core truths aren't negotiable, but neither are they the only thing happening in the world. The more you get in touch with your own core, the more you're able to make the space for others to do the same.

Knowing your truths doesn't require you to bludgeon the world with them. Once you've clearly shared them with others a few times, it will be on them whether they choose to accept and honor you. And if they don't, stand firm. There's no love or sense of security worth compromising your integrity for. You very well might have to leave an important relationship, either temporarily or permanently. You might have to learn to keep your heart open while others you love are angry with you. Whatever the hardship, honoring yourself will see you through, and when you do so, others will follow your lead.

Reveal, Don't Project

You've probably been on the other end of receiving someone else's projection of a stream of difficult emotions. Needless to say, it's not pleasant.

Most of us who've been taught to express our emotions fully haven't also been taught the difference between revealing our emotions and projecting them onto others. The distinction is between an invitation and an assault—an invitation to be present with a heart that's slowly widening to unveil painful emotions and an indiscriminate firehose rush upon another's nervous system. And so one key to leading and expressing your own Feminine is in learning how to open into difficult emotions without energetically pummeling other people with them.

Learning to identify, clarify, and reveal our anger, anguish, jealousy, and grief will make all the difference between our feelings being received as a gift as opposed to an attack. Take jealousy, for example, which can prove to be quite challenging to work with. The knee-jerk reaction when threatened with the fears of abandonment and rejection that come with being jealous is to relentlessly question others, accuse them, or completely withdraw. All of these responses are just as damaging to ourselves as they are to our partners. What if, instead, you could look straight into your lover's eyes, soften your heart, and say, "Oh baby, I am so jealous right now. I saw you talking and laughing with that guy, and I just wanted to come out of my skin." If communicating those feelings with words is difficult when you're activated, try instead to embody those feelings in ways that share your vulnerability with your partner.

PRACTICE INHALING JEALOUSY

The next time you experience the pangs of jealousy, try this with your partner. First, imagine inhaling the jealousy into your chest. Bring it into your heart on a smooth inhale, suspend your breath for a moment, and let the muscles of your heart soften around it. Then, on the next inhalation, imagine your entire body opening as wide as the jealousy itself—as wide as the room you're in, as wide as the entire neighborhood, as wide as the surrounding forest. Then speak to what's in your heart; for example, "Ouch, babe," or "I want to go punch that person," or "I want you all to myself, and the idea of another man's hands on you makes me crazy."

If your lover can experience you offering all of these feelings as you open wide—rather than you closing off in silence or blaming your partner for your pain—they will be drawn in and love you for it. I can attest to this by practicing this myself and watching countless men and women do the same.

Revealing difficult emotions in this way is one of the most important relationship skills we can master. Allowing your nervous system to relax open with all of that energy moving through you will pay dividends in your sex, your capacity to hold powerful feelings, and your ability to shepherd and nurture the difficult emotions in others.

USE OTHER MEN TO SHARPEN YOUR SWORD

The Power of Men's Work

As I mentioned in the introduction, long ago I set an impossible goal to help create ten thousand men's groups around the world. It didn't matter to me that the number was probably unattainable; I knew that transforming the collective masculine consciousness was going to require some lofty thinking.

Men need support in order to grow and gain capacity as leaders, and they need containers for embodied practice. They need spaces to drop into their own vulnerability, and they need to be held by kind others as they learn to heal and integrate. Men need sanctuaries to reset their nervous systems, and friends who ask nothing from them but the truth. They need to receive the wisdom of their brothers—wisdom born of genuine depth and pristine consciousness. Men need sacred halls in which the lost rituals of manhood are reborn and reimagined for the modern experience. They need safe circles in which to reveal their fears, insecurities, and yearnings, and they need a community of other men to offer their hearts and honest feedback. People of all genders and inclinations need these things, too (or at least some of them), but in this section I'm speaking especially to and for people who identify as men.

The type of men's groups I have in mind are oases of stillness and clarity in a speedy world of mindless, nonstop striving. In these groups, men can finally experience the kind of masculine fullness and love that penetrates their hearts and challenges them at their cores. Men are starving for this. Men crave a new paradigm—a new way of relating to each other beyond the approved venues of sporting events and bars. For generations now, we have become more and more disconnected from the land, from the infinite source of life, and from the circles of wisdom that for so long fed us and provided guidance and support through life's trials. There have been countless imitations, but most of them have fallen short, at best. Religious factions, secret societies, exclusive (and typically whites-only) clubs—all of these have only served to proliferate dogma and dominate those outside of the chosen group, namely nonwhites and women. With few exceptions, most of what has passed for "men's groups" has had very little to do with actual liberation.

Men need their core depth reflected back to them through the eyes of other men.

For millennia, men have sat together in circles in times of peace and before, during, and after stressful events like war. They relaxed within the container, shared stories of their experiences, offered their wisdom and support, and received physiological and spiritual nourishment from their brothers. And they also were the recipients of a form of masculine love not easily found in today's world—a love as fiercely challenging as it is connective and affectionate. Men journeyed alongside each other in complete recognition, whether it be through the threats of famine and war or through the transformative practices and rituals of manhood. Men recognized each other as conscious love, while simultaneously demanding that everyone in the circle give their all to the world from that fundamental truth.

In short, men need their core depth reflected back to them through the eyes of other men. It changes a man. It restores him. It inspires him to elevate himself and give more than he knew was possible. I have seen the visceral impact of this on a man's nervous system for years now. It is a palpable, relaxed sharpening that straightens his spine and opens his heart. One that not only elevates him but is felt by others and shared with them when he returns home to his family and community.

Healing the Father Wound in a Brotherhood of Men

Like far too many men, I grew up without the presence of a strong father figure. Sadly, we have now been witness to two or three generations of an increasing number of men who grew up without the necessary presence of fathers in their lives.

The masculine imprint we receive as a child stays with us and becomes the prism through which we see the Masculine in the world—in other individual men we know, in groups of men, in our leaders, and in other cultural representatives or structures of authority—and often that imprint is marked with neglect, detachment, rage, self-centeredness, or murky relationship to the Feminine. And even if we were fortunate enough to have caring and attentive father figures, there's still likely some piece of masculinity missing due to the shortcomings of the world we live in.

That being the case, most of us carry some father wound that can't help but play out in our relationships with other men or anything that feels like masculine structure to us. Authority issues are a perfect manifestation of this. It can also show up as a subtle mistrust or fear of confrontation with other men. Whatever the wound, you'll be able to trace it in your relationships in the ways you're habitually disappointed or triggered.

My primary Daddy complaint was that he didn't show up and do the work he needed to grow. So, what happens when the men around me don't show up and do the work? That wound gets triggered, which is understandably an issue for someone like me (that is, a teacher of men's work). Fortunately, I noted the tendency early on, so whenever it arises now I'm able to own it and use it as a teaching point. But to do so I had to first recognize the wound and accept that it was going to show up with other men. That's what it takes to untie the knot.

If you are surrounded by other men who are aware enough to know that changing the collective masculine psyche involves a ton of individual men doing the work, then you are fortunate to be in a space where there can be a massive healing around the masculine wound. It might start with you and the men in your group owning your father wounds and how they show up in your life, or it may involve practices designed to free you and your father (and maybe even your son) from the generational patterns and pains received from our grandfathers—overwork, abandonment, rage, treating others as a burden, and so on.

Whatever the masculine imprint, a solid men's group will provide your nervous system and heart with the safety to move through the grief, rage, and disappointment you've been carrying. There is a specific healing power in bringing your father wound to light and sharing it in the company of loving men. Rather than numbing out or ignoring the pain, your brothers make transmutation possible, which means that your wound becomes your ally, and that ally will help you free other men. You might not have bought this book out of an inspiration to heal other men, but I assure you that sharing your process and love with others who have battled similar disappointments can be one of the most rewarding experiences in life.

Healing your father wound will strengthen your nervous system, support your core, and empower you as an authentic leader in your world.

You'll be better able to recognize imprints in the act and reduce their impact on others, including your lovers and your children. You'll be able to confront other men lovingly and honestly. You'll face your own truths without collapsing. And, most importantly, you'll free yourself from the karmic bondage of your father's limitations. You'll finally become your own man. To that end, I invite you to try a powerful practice to help you begin the journey of healing this wound.

PRACTICE **WRITING TO YOUR FATHER**

While you may never deliver them, I want you to write two letters to your father. In the first, thank him profusely for all that he gave you—any positive traits, memories, gifts, and life lessons. Speak as cleanly and as openly as possible, steering clear of any passive aggression or criticism of any kind. Just praise and gratitude.

In the second letter, do the exact opposite—I want you to hold nothing back. Tell him, in detail, all about your sadness, your disappointment, your anger, and your confusion. Every time he hurt you, hurt your family, hurt himself. The ways he may have checked out, abandoned, and neglected you. Truly open your heart and let it fly. After you've finished both letters, share them with your men's group or a trusted friend.

What you do with these letters isn't as important as the act of writing them. Feel free to burn them, drop them into the ocean, or bury them in the forest. Do whatever helps you feel a sense of completion, including reading the first letter to your father (if you're able).

Seek Men of Depth

You may have a number of good friends—guys you've known from college or childhood who you've loved all of your life. You might also be blessed with hunting or sports buddies, or men you regularly play video games with from around the world. All of that's great, but it's not the same thing as having men of depth in your life.

What I'm referring to are men connected to their core truth. These are men you should befriend and learn from. These are also the men who will see through your stories and destroy your illusions about what you think you know about life. So, if there's a man you know who has something of essence, perhaps something you yearn for and lack, seek him out. Maybe there's a man in your circle whose love for his wife is way more profound than you believe yourself capable of. Talk to him. Try to understand how he's able to access those places in his heart. Or maybe you know a man who is intimately connected to the divine, nature, or stillness. Ask him about his practice. What can he teach you? What myths can he dispel for you? Or perhaps you know a man who embodies his sexuality in a manner you believe to be beyond your capacities. Go learn what he has to share and level up.

The best athletes are often those who seek out the most challenging opponents. That's what it takes to hone their skills and master their art. Scour your world for men who will slay your ego with the power of their awareness and love. Find the men whose mere presence is a blessing, who encourage the stillness within you simply by encountering their stillness. Who inspires you to show your heart? Who encourages your nervous system to relax? We tend to assume the traits of the people we're in contact with the most, so make the men in your life count. The more you're around men who have cultivated their stillness, presence, and open-heartedness, the more you'll foster your own expression of the same.

Receive Nourishment from Other Men

There's a unique form of nourishment men receive from playing, meditating, and practicing with other men. It's a form of embodied wisdom, and I see it regularly in the retreats I lead, particularly when men get to go out into nature together. Something shifts in them. Their nervous systems begin to co-regulate, supported by the rhythms and wisdom of the natural world. As men, we need this, and it's something we can't do alone.

Enjoying play with other men and "bro-ing out" is a wonderful aspect of the masculine experience, but we're missing out if that's as far as our relationships with other men go. Men also need the nourishment that only comes from challenging each other and finding stillness together, that's only possible when we hold each other to more noble and powerful standards of being. When a man practices holding pristine presence with another man, while being challenged to go deeper into himself, it stretches his capacities—particularly his awareness—and empowers him to transmit his best into the world. This in itself is incredibly nourishing.

And when another man who cares for him witnesses his struggle and the opening of his core, he becomes stronger than he ever thought possible. His nervous system becomes more resilient and pliable, and he will walk in the world supported by the love of his brothers.

> Consciousness sharpens consciousness.
> Integrity sharpens integrity. Feeling
> inspires and evokes more feeling.

It's the same practice that warriors, yogis, shamans, and martial artists have engaged in for ages. Most men today have been so habituated to comfort and ease that we believe they're synonymous with nourishment, but the fact is that our nervous systems are designed to thrive in hardship and the face of challenge, as well as in the company of trusted others. Our Feminine side may be nourished by equally as important things (praise, for example), but our Masculine aspect requires clear challenges to thrive.

PRACTICE GET TO THE CORE OF IT

The next time you're out having a few beers with your buddies or shooting the shit about girlfriends or work, try this practice out. In conversation, bring up what's most important for you at this moment of your life. Tell your friends what you want to do before you die. Speak to your fear; give voice to your mission in life. And then let yourself be seen and witnessed. Let them give you feedback on where they think your commitment is lacking—maybe even solicit their help for an action plan. It may nourish you in a way you've never truly let other men offer you (or that you've never let these particular men offer you). It may relax something in you to reveal a core truth and be met with their presence and acceptance, and maybe—if they're men of depth— even grant you a little smack to help you pull your head out of your ass. All of these things will enliven you and spark your hormonal and nervous systems to bring you out of your lethargy and prepare you to return to the world alive, openhearted, and full of masculine nourishment.

Iron Sharpens Iron

There's a saying from Proverbs in the Hebrew Bible that's usually translated as *iron sharpens iron*. Most of us have come to associate this axiom with physical strength and mental toughness, as in it takes a strong man to "sharpen" another strong man, or it takes a tough man to make another man tougher. This is true, of course, but it goes way beyond that.

Consciousness sharpens consciousness. Integrity sharpens integrity. Feeling inspires and evokes more feeling. Depth breeds more depth. Clarity begets clarity.

This is the beauty of men's work. It's like CrossFit for your spiritual and emotional masculine development. Sure, physical challenge and play will help strengthen a man's body and nervous system, but ask him to sit in front of another man, look him dead in the eyes, and hold him to a higher level of conscious presence for thirty minutes. Watch his consciousness sharpen before you. Witness his awareness and capacity for presence shoot through the proverbial roof.

Have two men commit to cleaning up integrity lapses with each other for thirty days, and each will sharpen their awareness around their words, deeds, and actions. Have two men practice expanding their feeling awareness together—feeling below them, above them, and all around them (all while maintaining eye contact)—and their feeling capacity will expand dramatically. Now add some kind of physical challenge (holding a qigong pose, for example), and you create a powerful cocktail of masculine practice that amplifies his nervous system, awareness, and feeling capacities exponentially. Top it off by having him relax his heart while enduring the physical and energetic strain. And then notice how his iron is sharpened.

Ask for Bold Feedback

One of the ways we can sharpen our own awareness is to ask other men what they think and feel about our presence, integrity, and conduct in our lives. The deeper and more grounded the men, the more valuable their feedback, just as we might seek from professional mentors. We invite their consciousness in to help us scrape off the dull edges of our comfortable lives, and we seek their assistance in cutting through our delusions by shining the light of their awareness on our shadows, detrimental habits, and self-centered patterns.

This is how we craft a new paradigm of men's practice together: one conversation at a time, one challenge at a time, one clear piece of truth at a time. I did this for eight years, nearly every Monday night, with a group of men that became my council. Everything worthwhile and good in my life has been washed, purified, and made available to others through the wisdom and kindness of these men (including this book). For years they listened to me whine about my responsibilities and complain about not having enough free time, especially when I was clocking so many hours in the hospital with my daughter. Week after week, these men would lovingly remind me that my deepest practice was to face death with my daughter and remain open to growing and cleaning up any gray areas as a man. That meant reducing the amount of time I was devoting to teaching men's work. They suggested I limit myself to only one teaching slot a month, and they challenged me to walk the talk by spending the rest of my time in authentic practice. It was difficult advice to follow, but they were right.

When my daughter turned eighteen, I started teaching a lot more, and I even started taking her with me when I traveled to Europe. She loved that, and I'm so glad I did it. Everything in life that I am proud of — including reducing my teaching commitments to devote more time to my daughter in the last three years of her life — I can trace back to those men and their unflinching wisdom and feedback. I'll be forever grateful to them for that.

PRACTICE **HOLDING COUNCIL WITH OTHER MEN**

Here's a practice I learned from Deida years ago. Set up periodic councils with your men's group in which you unveil what you're currently up against. Allow time for them to offer feedback, and take it all in. They might cheer you on, firmly remind you of stated priorities, or tell you you're full of shit. They might point out tendencies about yourself you'd rather not have pointed out, but that's the whole reason for the practice. Iron isn't known for sharpening itself.

Let your brothers pierce your ego and touch your heart. Let them hone your awareness and bring out the best in you. Have them offer you a challenge or practice or commitment you must take on and complete. Set up a clear accountability with them, with considerable consequences should you flake out. Consider their suggestions, and when it's your turn, offer them your own. Often the most helpful solutions are those offered from outside the habituated confines of our own thinking, and men's groups can offer unparalleled support when it comes to learning new and more grounded ways to lead ourselves, our relationships, and our world.

Become a Leader of Men

In the journey of honing your skills as a practitioner—strengthening your nervous system, sharpening your consciousness, learning to open your heart, and expanding your capacity to feel and express your core truths—you'll probably want to share your growth and process with other men. Do it. Start a men's group of your own. Take the lead in your spiritual community and encourage your fellow men to get honest and embodied. Whether in the realm of politics, parenting, martial arts, or your spiritual practice, take the principles you have picked up here and make a stand for other men.

There's something transformative that occurs when you step out of the role of student (or dabbler) and try on the big-boy pants of a leader. They often won't feel like they fit, especially as you grow into all of the challenges that leadership brings, but each test you face will ultimately make you a more powerful man. Your capacity to move from practitioner to teacher will expand you in every direction: you'll become clearer, more focused, and more on point. And you'll learn to penetrate the hearts of other men with your core truths, deepen your presence, and feel more fully into the moment while also remaining rooted in something greater than yourself.

Where you want to take your newly heightened skills of awareness and feeling is up to you. Maybe you want to fight for social justice or help alleviate climate disruption or teach men practices to help them become more embodied. Maybe there's a cause aligned with your company that could use your expertise and focus. Maybe there are men in your life who need assistance with all the challenges that parenting and partnership can bring. Whatever it is, your masculine aspect will grow in the fire as you take your stand and lead other men down the path. So, find where your depth is most needed and dive in.

The Feminine Trusts Men
Who Other Men Trust

Leadership is a trait that the Feminine has appreciated and craved from the Masculine throughout time, whether those masculine figures were tribal leaders, warriors, spiritual teachers, business leaders, or fathers. Being funny or handsome has its place, but it doesn't compare to being an effective and respected leader in the community with the power and capacity to keep others (and the children of others) safe. That's the sort of thing that truly elevates your value as a protector, ally, and mate. When others depend on you (especially other men) and you turn out to be noble and dependable, it's a big turn-on.

If you apply the principles I've laid out for you to your relationships with other men, you'll become more present, open, grounded, conscious, loving, and capable of facing life's storms, and other men will take notice, seek you out, and want to know more about what the fuck you're doing. I see it happen all the time these days, as more and more are recognizing the power of grounded presence and conscious depth, seeking it out in droves. There's a sea change happening in men—especially when it comes to redefining what masculinity means in today's age—and I invite you to do what you can to get the other men in your life on board. And when you do, watch how feminine beings in your life begin to take notice.

MAKE DEATH
AN ALLY

Death Is Coming

We're all going to die. That much is obvious. But aside from accepting this fact somewhat remotely, our relationship to death is largely avoidant or fearful. By and large, most men's relationship to their mortality is either feeble or uninspiring.

Making death an ally requires you to constantly align your life decisions as if death were near. Doing so, you can take advantage of the inevitable end as a purifying, clarifying, and energizing force. Think about how your thoughts and mood would change if you knew you were going to die tomorrow. How much attention, love, and commitment would you bring to what would surely be your last acts on earth? How present, grateful, and awe-inspired would you be? Consider how you'd kiss your lover, put your child to bed, prepare your last meal, or take your final walk in the woods.

In truth, we can die at any moment of any day. More people than you think will die today from car accidents, complications from routine surgeries, aneurisms, and so on, and none of them were expecting it in the least. So why not consider it for yourself? Whether it's today, tomorrow, next year, or forty years from now, your death is coming anyway.

Let go of petty grudges. Get off your ass. Focus on the people who truly matter. Think about all the things you'd like to say or accomplish before you leave this realm. What needs to happen so that you can die complete? What will it take to ensure you won't be one of those people with a list of deathbed regrets? Get clear on whatever it is and let that dictate the rest of your life. And since priorities naturally change over time, make sure to make this inquiry an ongoing and integral part of your life. Let death be your ally and advisor.

ONE OF THE unexpected gifts of raising a child with a terminal illness is the inability to escape the inevitability of death. We thought Claire was going to die multiple times before she actually did. When she was thirteen, my daughter went into a three-week-long coma that changed all of our lives. When Claire miraculously emerged with a new lease on life (albeit a more challenging one), her mother and I knew that we had to make friends with Claire's death. We had to prepare for what was coming, and a culture of understanding grew around us. Because things could go south at any moment, we consistently asked, "What needs to happen for Claire to have the life of her dreams?" After the coma, she wanted to go to Sitka, Alaska, so we went. She wanted to start a foundation for kids with cystic fibrosis, so we did that, too. Claire gave three TED talks and traveled around the world speaking on behalf of other children with special needs. I took her with me on teaching trips to Europe, flying first class when I could afford it, and we swam with dolphins in Hawaii. We packed sixty years of living into the last six years of her life. Of everything I've done in life, I'll always be proudest of that. Every time we reached a fork in the road, we considered her death. Either things were conducive to helping her die with a sense of completion, or they weren't. Of course, we couldn't give her everything, but we were able to align our priorities so that when Claire did die, we'd know we did our damnedest, and she had lived as fully as possible.

Maybe it's easier to make death an ally when it's your child on the line. Maybe there's something about the nature of that loss that makes the whole thing choiceless. But is it really all that different for you and me? Death is coming for all of us. It's happening to somebody right now in the form of a drunk driver, an unexpected heart attack, or a stray blood clot. Why not you?

Get clear on your priorities and let them shape your life. Cut out the bullshit. When death comes, it doesn't have to be a tragedy. In fact, knowing your death is on its way can be one of life's greatest blessings. To that end, here are four empowering practices for conscious dying.

PRACTICE WRITING YOUR EULOGY

What would you like people to say at your funeral? Write it out in detail or ask a friend to do it. The trick here is not just to include all the high points but also every regret and unmet desire you can think of. Use this writing assignment to take stock of your life from birth to the present moment, and really imagine it's over—you're dead. Read what you wrote and see what comes up. The good news is that you're not dead yet, so you can use your eulogy to make whatever life adjustments seem necessary. Share the practice with your men's group and ask them to hold you to your commitments to change your life accordingly.

PRACTICE **MEDITATING ON DEATH**

Spiritual practitioners have been doing some form of this meditation for thousands of years. After breathing mindfully for some time, choose a final breath and empty your lungs of air. Hold that pose. When the urge to inhale comes, consider that it might not. Imagine that there's not another breath, that this is the moment of your death. Relax into the thoughts and sensations that arise for as long as you can, and then let them fade away and dissolve. Whatever comes up—hopes, panic, dreams, goals, regrets—let it vanish and return to the earth.

PRACTICE **TUNING IN TO THE DEATH THAT SURROUNDS YOU**

Feel out into your environment. Somewhere close by, insects, plants, small animals, large ones, and even some other human not too far off is currently dying. Can you feel it? Not just as some morbid last gasp, but as the beautiful and necessary transition of the cosmos. Continue sensing out around the world to where death and life are endlessly dancing together—in the great oceans, deserts, and redwood forests. Carry your awareness out into space, where planets are dying and black holes are swallowing up entire solar systems. Don't turn away. Feel death's presence as an integrated part of existence. What relaxation, clarity, or purity arises for you when you approach death this way?

PRACTICE **REFLECTING EVERY NIGHT**

Every night we fall into a faux death state in which we slip out of waking consciousness and let go of our lives. We can use the moments before falling asleep to contemplate our death or, rather, our life. Before dropping into sleep, reflect on what needed to happen today for you to let go of life and have no regrets. Did you leave some important project unfinished? Did you take the time to engage in nourishing activities for yourself? Did you tell your kids you loved them? What are you most proud of? If you don't feel that you can die tonight knowing that your day was beautifully executed, wake up tomorrow and try again. Pick three things to focus on. I'm not talking about making another to-do list of mundane tasks; I'm talking about three action items that would eat away at you if you didn't complete them tomorrow.

The power and freedom that comes from bringing death into your daily life in these ways is astounding. You'll have way more energy because you'll be increasingly aligned with your core truths. You'll also sleep like a baby. And prioritizing life's never-ending tasks and duties won't be such a hassle because you'll know what you need to do to live with maximum integrity.

Feel Death as the Masculine

If the Feminine expresses as all phenomena and energy manifesting, moving, growing, and flourishing in the cosmos (galaxies being born, snow melting, flowers blossoming, and so on), then the polar opposite can be found in the absence of movement, in nothingness and in death. Consider death as the ultimate Masculine expression. I'm not referring to sickness, decay, or murder here—those are all still aspects of life. Instead, think about the *absence* of life—the cessation of movement and being. Feel the utter completeness of that, the infinite truth. If the divine is the complete expression of both manifest and latent realities, then life is the manifest expression (the Feminine) and death is the latent truth (the Masculine).

Bringing more awareness to the endings of things enriches our experience. We're able to relax and open in new and surprising ways. We know the wonderful party is coming to a close, we see the end of an incredible love affair in sight, and we're increasingly aware that our life will one day be over—perhaps a lot sooner than we'd like. One uniquely beautiful moment fades and another rises to replace it.

Don't let death go to waste. Don't turn your face away from it. Make death your friend and ally; use it to infuse your world with gratitude and make this life a celebration. Death is coming; your end is coming. That's where awe, wonder, and gratefulness come from. Without death, life wouldn't be anything special.

THE PRECEPTS OF CONSCIOUS WARRIORHOOD

MY INTENTION HAS been for you to finish this book with an inspired understanding of what it means to live from the space of expanded awareness and love — in a state of conscious warriorhood. There is a tremendous amount of energy and inspiration a man receives when he taps into his Warrior within — he straightens his spine, sharpens his gaze, and clears his mind. The conscious warrior has no interest in domination or adding suffering to the world, but wields his (or her) strength, aptitude, fierceness, and nobility in service of liberating consciousness and amplifying love.

Relying on the innovations of ancient yogic, meditative, and martial arts traditions, he cultivates the skills of presence, clarity, and integrity as weapons against lethargy, apathy, and numbness, applying them to his own life first, and then to the world around him. This way of living requires consistent reflection and practice. It will not happen on its own — the pull of modern life toward accumulation, consumption, and numbness is just too strong.

Throughout the ages, warriors have lived by sets of rules, tenets, and creeds. Although this was true for the samurai and the romanticized Knights of the Round Table, these warriors were still subject to decrees of power and domination. The precepts of conscious warriorhood are quite different. And they're meant to recognize and repair the fact that men, in particular, have been bringing their strength and fierceness to the wrong battles for the wrong reasons for tens of thousands of years.

That must change. We are at a critical moment of history in which technological development, social inequities, environmental devastation, and climate disruption are all colliding. Men are now being called to move beyond a simple rallying in opposition to political, social, and economic crises, and to apply their skills and strengths to supporting the rise of the Feminine, the elevation of consciousness, and the liberation of love. What this looks like in your life will be different from someone else's, but I have found a structure to consistently contemplate and live by to be incredibly helpful.

Remember, everything I've offered in this book is meant as a practice. There's actually nothing to perfect or complete here, but instead a lifelong set of guidelines and poses to try out, open into, and grow with.

The precepts I'm about to outline distill all of this book's material in eleven principles you can apply to your life right now. They affect not just your living experience but the world's experience of you as well. Apply them to your relationships, your work in the world, your purpose, and every space you enter.

Feel into which precepts already hold a firm place in your awareness and which are elusive or challenging to apply. Continue to hone those you already feel grounded in and make a commitment to strengthen those that feel difficult or out of reach. By doing so, you'll become a leader in the liberation of love and the elevation of consciousness in the world.

PRACTICE CONTEMPLATING THE PRECEPTS

Choose one precept per day and meditate on it for five minutes. Try turning them into questions, for example, "Where can I be more ruthlessly honest with myself, while also practicing kindness with others?" See what comes up for you. Where have you been dishonest, delusional, or naive? Where have you been fooling yourself? Where have you needlessly attacked others because you felt shitty or trapped or victimized? Scan your current experience for where you can apply your answers and visualize yourself living from the core of these precepts. Let your nervous system experience what it's like to see yourself deepening into this way of life. What might be different, more expansive, and more nourishing? Where might others be able to trust you more? Most importantly, how different would you feel about yourself?

Once you have clearly determined an area to improve on, make a commitment to do something in service of that precept. Are there apologies to make? Spaces to transform with your meticulous attention? Certain practices to take on or return to? Whatever it is, choose to place your attention and effort in that direction. Over the course of time, your capacity to deliver in the areas that matter most will expand dramatically, and your life will grow accordingly.

Please do not underestimate the power of living in this way. Small wins in this fashion will deliver what you crave most: peace, fulfillment, abundance, and love. I'm not promising more money, greater success, or less responsibility—I'm talking about what matters most *in your core*.

Eleven Precepts of Conscious Warriorhood

The Conscious Warrior is ruthlessly honest with himself while being kind to others.

The Conscious Warrior cultivates impeccability in his presence, his environment, his way of being, and his way in the world.

The Conscious Warrior prioritizes the creation of an unshakable tether to consciousness, stillness, and depth.

The Conscious Warrior is committed to feeling deeply rather than numbing or succumbing to comfort or addiction.

The Conscious Warrior takes 100 percent responsibility for the reality he has created—seeking what needs to be changed in him before blaming others.

The Conscious Warrior is committed to developing strength of mind, body, and nervous system through dedicated physical, yogic, and meditative practice.

The Conscious Warrior practices the cultivation of wonder and awe.

The Conscious Warrior honors and protects the Feminine in himself, in women, in children, and in the world.

The Conscious Warrior is always deepening, always a student— seeking other men and teachers who will slay his ego and sharpen his consciousness.

The Conscious Warrior is continuously refining his deepest purpose through dedicated time in solitude and in the company of other men.

The Conscious Warrior makes death an ally, using it to sharpen his present actions, future plans, and current state of being.

Ode to My Brothers

For as long as you are alive, you will always think that you could be doing more. No matter your achievements, accomplishments, possessions, or experiences. Your partner may never stop commenting on your lack of presence, consistency of commitment, or support. They may never truly see your nobility, may never truly appreciate how hard you work, and may not give you the kind of sexual energy you crave. The people you love most may betray you, die, or not care. You will give your heart and soul to something only to have the world meet it with tepid approval. It may even be ignored completely. If you are successful, it will grant you but a momentary reprieve, and the inevitable feeling that you should be doing more will always win over the fleeting elation of meeting your goal. In fact, you may suffer a crisis of faith as the accrual of everything you were told would make you happy never quite quells the longing to express something of true impact. You will search for ways to numb this pain. Men will disappoint you with their lack of depth and consciousness; you will feel angry and want to shake them.

If you truly care about people and the world, they will inevitably break your heart. The cruelty, judgment, and violence we perpetrate on each other will rock you to your core. You will fall prey to addictions and distractions in a continued and fruitless attempt to ease or offset the pain of loneliness, boredom, or unfulfilled dreams. You will likely hate yourself for it, even though you might not admit it. Most days will feel like a burden, chasing a myth of success that you believe will finally get you somewhere and make you someone. You will ache for freedom, space, and time. You will ache for purpose, for greater impact, and to be seen for your valor and integrity. It will often elude you. At times, you'll feel helpless, hopeless, and alone. Don't deny any of it. Instead, feel all of it.

Simply allow the utter futility of your effort to break your heart. Let the pain of your failures, heartbreaks, sicknesses, and death crush you. Face your own inevitable demise. See your body—and with it, all your work on earth—in the ground. Relax fully, right now, into the sorrow of living until your shoulders drop and tears well up. Surrender completely to the inevitable, unfulfilled nature of your existence. Practice dying and let go of the misguided impulse to strive at all costs. Now you can begin.

Choose who you want to love and do so fiercely, with your wide-open, Grand Canyon heart. Let the weight of how much you love ripple over the surface of the world and penetrate deeply below. Create something that is uniquely yours with the unbendable intention of someone who is hell-bent on walking through a wall. Be meticulous in its creation. Let whatever it is be a monument to your truest heart and consciousness. Let the rest go. There just isn't enough time. Life is short and death is coming. Anyone not in support of or in alignment with your deepest purpose can fuck off.

Breathe in the remarkable and mundane beauty around you at every turn. Celebrate it when you can. Smile and bow with a grateful heart. Let go of tasks and duties and allow the Feminine to give you her love. Relax the center of your body and let her shine all that is good in the world upon your weary soul. Let her know how grateful you are. Play with children, yours and others, as if it is your last moment on earth, allowing your presence and love to inform the rest of their lives. It will.

Whatever you do, hold nothing back. Not one word of truth, not one ounce of love, not one word of wisdom, not one feeling left unfelt. Leave this world bloody and broken-hearted, smiling and grateful. Free as much love as possible along the way. Let your legacy be your grounded, embodied presence and your fierce, aching heart.

This is living from the core. And it's all that will matter in the end.

ACKNOWLEDGMENTS

I HAVE ENDEAVORED to live by the creed and teach only what I've practiced, embodied, and integrated. I have tried to write about what I've learned from a handful of amazing teachers over the past two decades of my life—and then taught—to as many men as I could. As such, I have massive gratitude for those who have taught me to expand my capacity and understanding of men's work, yogic intimacy, and spiritual practice. I have already mentioned David Deida and the framework of understanding and practice he has given me, but I also feel profound gratitude for his commitment to the purity of love and consciousness in the world and the way he has modeled living and giving his work.

I also want to thank Teo Alfero, who guided me for two years into the realm of understanding mysticism as masculine practice and how to integrate the two. Sifu Matthew Klein and his Martial Arts of Wellness teachings have been invaluable, not only to my personal practice but also as a philosophy to draw and innovate from. Cass Phelps and his remarkable understanding of the flow of energy, breath, openness, and power has also had a profound impact on my thinking, teaching, and life. A deep bow to you all.

For over a decade, I have been blessed to be in men's groups with incredible brothers and teachers, all of whom have deepened and sharpened me. They held me through grief that was unimaginable and gave me the strength and ruthlessly compassionate feedback I needed to take care of my family, build my purpose, and live a dharma I could be proud of.

Thank you to my team, who have built and held our programs over the past five years, and to the people at Sounds True who helped me collate all of my material into something hopefully digestible and applicable. Thank you to Kelly Sue Mellano and her editing, suggestions, and holding of these writings.

Many thanks to my mother, who taught me about the Mystic Law of cause and effect and how to recite the Lotus Sutra when I was seven years old. From early in my life, she instilled in me the power and value of practice and prayer. It has been my daily practice for over forty years.

But most of all, this book is for my daughter, Claire, whose beautiful and heartbreaking life taught me everything I could want to know about love, death, and God. It is one thing to talk about staying open in the midst of pain and uncertainly, and something completely different to practice it in the face of death every day. She did so for years with grace, humor, and radiance—making art and inspiring others every step of the way. Thank you, Claire. You are the love of my life, and I miss you every day.

ABOUT THE AUTHOR

JOHN WINELAND IS a writer, teacher, and speaker who guides other people in the realms of life purpose, relational communication, sexual intimacy, and embodiment. John brings an energetic and highly practical approach to his workshops and experiential coaching sessions. His embodiment-driven teaching draws from his thirty-plus years of Buddhist meditative practice and over ten years of intensive study with renowned yogic intimacy teacher David Deida. Also drawing from Vajrayana Buddhism, Tantra, Kundalini Yoga, and Taoist and Iron Shirt Qigong traditions, John seeks to create a profound experience for people who long to express their deepest desires with open, fierce, and loving hearts. See more at JohnWineland.com.

ABOUT SOUNDS TRUE

SOUNDS TRUE IS a multimedia publisher whose mission is to inspire and support personal transformation and spiritual awakening. Founded in 1985 and located in Boulder, Colorado, we work with many of the leading spiritual teachers, thinkers, healers, and visionary artists of our time. We strive with every title to preserve the essential "living wisdom" of the author or artist. It is our goal to create products that not only provide information to a reader or listener but also embody the quality of a wisdom transmission.

For those seeking genuine transformation, Sounds True is your trusted partner. At SoundsTrue.com you will find a wealth of free resources to support your journey, including exclusive weekly audio interviews, free downloads, interactive learning tools, and other special savings on all our titles.

To learn more, please visit SoundsTrue.com/freegifts or call us toll-free at 800.333.9185.